OLD CLEEVE PA

Jeanne Webb

2003

Millennium Awards

TARKA·COUNTRY
MILLENNIUM AWARDS

March 2003

This guide has been funded by Tarka Country Millennium Awards using Lottery money through the Millennium Commission.
The conditions of the Award are such that the project has to be seen to benefit the community as well as the Award Winner. The Award Winner is prohibited from personal financial gain from the project. The book is available at a low cost and all monies received from the sale of the guide will be reserved for a reprint should it be required, or after a fixed period, passed to Old Cleeve Parish Council to support a project of their choosing.

PREFACE

A special book for a special parish. That, in a nutshell is what this beautifully-written, well-researched collection must represent to any lover of the West Somerset countryside. Let me explain, briefly, why I make such a claim.

As a professional walks-writer for the main daily newspaper in the West Country, I receive many parish footpath guides and I have no hesitation in saying that this is the best example of the genre I've seen. Secondly, as an Old Cleeve parish councillor, I am aware of the fact that our public rights-of-way need all the promotion and press they can get. Nothing is more detrimental to the health of a footpath than neglect and lack of use.

Not only is Old Cleeve one of the largest parishes in the region, it is one of the most diverse. Few parishes in the country contain such a range of countryside – from the 1,200 foot Brendon Hill escarpment in the south, to the fossil-bearing reefs of the Bristol Channel in the north. We have forests, and we have tiny copses; we have meandering streams and mighty waterfalls; high grasslands and luxuriant, impenetrable, thickets. There is limestone, sandstone and slate; and there are hamlets that appear untouched by the passing of time and we also have a busy main-road village.

Into this great demesne marched Jeanne Webb. Armed with a great love of this most beautiful of areas – and an observant eye – she has walked o'er hill and dale making notes, recording the flora and fauna and noting the idiosyncrasies of this footpath and that. The result is this attractively-presented affordable book. The Assessment Panel of the Tarka Country Millennium Awards Scheme said the project would "fill a gap in the existing provision of information for walkers." 1 believe it does that in the most entertaining and informative of ways.

It can only be hoped that parishioners and visitors alike will be inspired to march forth along our 71 footpaths, clutching this book as they go. As a guide, it will - for many years to come - act as an invaluable companion to all those who love the parish of Old Cleeve.

Martin Hesp

Ille te mecum locus et beatae postulant arces

"This place and these happy hills call out to you and me."

Horace, Odes, Book 2 : 6.

ACKNOWLEDGEMENTS

I am grateful to the Tarka Country Millenium Awards Scheme which has financed my project from its conception to completion, also to Old Cleeve Parish Council who have supported me throughout.

Alison Kent from Exmoor National Park Authority, who first suggested I applied for Tarka funding, and Adrian Fowler from West Somerset District Council have assisted when required, helping and encouraging me through the various stages.

Winsford Computer Centre's teaching staff increased my understanding of the properties and complexities of the computer. Paul Roberts and Jim Kent provided vital practical assistance in the later stages for which I am most grateful.
I thank Friday Print for their patience and professionalism.

Every walk has been checked on the ground for accuracy of information and a number of friends have undertaken this task with cheerful enthusiasm :
    Kieran Boulton, Paul Roberts, Gerald and Tessa Stowell,
    Simon Webb and Jean Johnston, John and Margaret West.
 I am indebted to them all for their valuable assistance, especially the one among their number who carefully proof-read the ever-growing manuscript. I thank Tessa Stowell for her contribution and Philippa Gerry for checking the finer points of the finished product.

Finally, without the help of my husband Tim, who walked every step of the way with me, it might have been something of a problem rather than the absolute pleasure that I have found in every one of the processes required in the production of this guide.
The benefit I have received is unquantifiable – hours of satisfaction in a place I love.
I hope those who walk these paths will find the same serenity and an equal pleasure.   J. W.

LIST OF ILLUSTRATIONS

Cover photograph ~
Ramsons, Allium ursinum, on the footpath between the Mineral Line and Ham Lane, the road to Leighland, on Walk No. 14.

Photographs and Illustrations by the author.

CONTENTS

INTRODUCTION

The guide includes all of the 71 rights-of-way that make up the footpaths of Old Cleeve Parish.
6 of these are classed as 'short-cuts' and cannot be included in a circular walk. Details of these are given on page 6.

There are 24 walks and each is graded :
- EASY (mostly level and short)
- MODERATE (a little longer with modest uphill stretches)
- CHALLENGING (longer, uphill and/or difficult terrain)

Each walk is circular (apart from Walk No. 24), has a special feature and the distance given. It is timed as a guide only – your fitness and mood being the deciding factors.
The walks are generally short but it is easy to join two or more together to make longer walks.

The parish can be divided roughly into three areas. Wherever you live or stay you are within reach of a number of walks that do not require transport to reach the start point:
Old Cleeve, Chapel Cleeve, Blue Anchor, Bilbrook & Washford
- Walk Nos. 1, 2, 3, 4, 5, 6, 7, 8,
Golsoncott, Croydon & Roadwater
- Walk Nos. 9, 10, 11, 12, 13, 14, 16, 17
Leighland & Brendon Hill
- Walk Nos.18, 19, 20, 21, 22, 23.
Walks No. 15 and 24 require transport.

🚐 Denotes suggestions for parking a vehicle, although there are a limited number of ideal places.
Buses travel from the A39 to Roadwater and beyond and also to Old Cleeve and Blue Anchor. Timetables can be obtained from Tourist Information offices and Traveline 0870 6082608.
Information and train times for the West Somerset Railway can also be obtained from stations and the 24-hour Talking Timetable 01643 707650.

1

Wheelchairs are permitted on footpaths although in practice there are few places where it is possible for them to make forward progress. Where there is a level section of path or a viewpoint is accessible the wheelchair sign is displayed in a box. Bridleways (footpaths which permit horses) are a better option because they have gates instead of stiles and it is surprising the sort of ground that can be accommodated by motorised wheelchairs. A pushchair has the advantage that both it and the occupant can be lifted over obstacles.

Descriptions of flowers, birds and mammals are given for those found at the particular time the walk was researched. This date is noted at the end of the text. Walks done at different times will more than likely record a different flora and fauna. However, whenever the walks are undertaken, something interesting is sure to be found.

All starting points have a six-figure number, which is the GRID REFERENCE. These are based on the Ordnance Survey maps, 'Explorer' or 'Outdoor Leisure', 2½ ins. to the mile, 4 cm. to 1 km. To find the grid reference look at the edge of the map where the vertical and horizontal gridlines are marked and further divided into unnumbered tenths.
The first 3 digits of the grid reference are calculated from left to right with the 3rd one an estimate of the tenths - this is the easting.
The second three digits are from bottom to top with the last digit again being an estimation of the position – this is the northing.
The grid reference is where the northing and easting cross.

For many walkers, satisfaction is incomplete without the companionship of their dog. Although your dog may have a long and exemplary record of good behaviour amongst farm animals, the animals are not aware of this and there have been occasions when stock has been injured after taking fright when dogs have merely shown curiosity.
For the dog's sake and for your peace of mind, the dog must not only be under control but be seen to be so, which means on a lead.

FOOTPATH INFORMATION

Every effort has been made to ensure the routes of paths are correct. The instructions for each have been checked for accuracy by a number of independent walkers.

No liability or responsibility can be accepted for the actions of people following the routes given, or for any accident or injury that may occur whilst so doing.

If you find any problem with any of the footpaths in Old Cleeve parish, other than those mentioned in this guide, please report them to the appropriate authority :
>   Somerset County Council : Tel. 01823 355604

If the paths are in Exmoor National Park : Tel. 01398 323665
The footpath identification numbers printed at Appendix 2 are the method by which paths are numbered within the local authority area. The list gives an approximate location only but it would be useful if you can quote the number when reporting the difficulty.
> e.g. WL 18/55
> WL - Williton,   18 - Old Cleeve parish,   55 - footpath number.

I hope you enjoy travelling the well-trodden paths as well as discovering the unknown parts of Old Cleeve parish.

Please cherish its beautiful places by always remembering the Country Code ~
> Enjoy the country and respect its life and work
> Guard against all risk of fire
> Fasten all gates
> Keep dogs under control
> Keep to public footpaths across all farmland
> Use gates and stiles to cross over field boundaries
> Leave all livestock, machinery and crops alone
> Take your litter home
> Help to keep all water clean
> Protect wildlife, plants and trees
> Make no unnecessary noise

TOPOGRAPHY

Old Cleeve Parish stretches from the seashore at Blue Anchor to Naked Boy's Stone on the ridge of the Brendon Hills. The parish covers an area of roughly 5,500 acres, two thirds of which lie within the area designated as Exmoor National Park.

GEOLOGY

At Blue Anchor the rocks are formed from late Triassic and early Jurassic mudstone with the cliffs containing a variety of fossils. Old Cleeve itself is underlain by marls with gravel deposits at Claydown Hill. The floodplains of the River Pill and the Washford River are made up of alluvial deposits. Triassic sandstones are found in the centre of the parish and pebble beds near Lodge Farm, with narrow bands of limestone outcropping near Golsoncott and Roadwater. The southern slopes of the Brendon Hills demonstrate Middle Devonian slates, siltstone and sandstones and south of Leigh Barton, Upper Devonian slates, siltstones and sandstones. Iron ore deposits come from the Devonian rocks and were extensively mined.

DRAINAGE

The Washford River drains the seaward facing slopes of the Brendon Hills, the east branch rising above Comberow, the west above Luxborough. The two tributaries unite at Roadwater, flow down to Cleeve Abbey and onwards through Washford eventually entering the sea at Watchet. The smaller River Pill rises above Rodhuish, flows down to the floodplain west of Old Cleeve and enters the sea at Blue Anchor.

VEGETATION

The landscape is generally comprised of fields enclosed by hedges. The higher, southern part of the parish is more wooded especially around Comberow where conifers dominate the skyline. Mixed deciduous woodland is common adjacent to the farmland in small copses and woods such as Trowden Wood at Washford, Harper's Wood at Roadwater and Broadfield Wood at Leighland. Grassland is dominant, the underlying geology determining the pH of the soil. In the north near the coast, the limestone rock creates alkaline soil, the Devonian rocks of the Brendon Hills create acidic.

The flora is as diverse as the individual habitats and rich in many areas such as the limestone grassland of Cleeve Hill, the pastures that have been left for generations, the riverbanks, and floodplains. The woodland floor supports mosses, lichens and a variety of fungi.

MAN-MADE FEATURES

Exmoor is scattered with a great variety of stone monoliths – in our parish ancient Naked Boy's Stone guards the parish boundary. Hundreds of Mesolithic artefacts have been found at Cleeve Hill. A Neolithic axe was found at Roadwater, implements from the Bronze Age at Leighland and an Iron Age armlet at Roadwater. Roman finds include coins from Washford and a fibula (brooch) from Blue Anchor.

Much of the parish's history is linked to Cleeve Abbey, the best-preserved Cistercian monastic site in the country.

St. Andrew's church in Old Cleeve, made of red sandstone and local blue lias, has some Norman herringbone masonry but has been altered and added to from the 12th century onwards.

St. Giles' church serves Leighland. Smaller chapels, both Anglican and Methodist, are found in Washford and Roadwater.

Many of the thatched cottages, some dating from the early 15th century, as well as the Cleeve Abbey Granges are listed buildings. Mills, waterwheels, leats, limekilns and bridges scattered around in all parts of the parish add variety to the historical record.

The West Somerset Mineral Line, The Incline, the winding house, a vast number of closed mine shafts and remains of stations along the line illustrate the importance of the mining era to the later historical and architectural legacy of the parish.

The West Somerset Railway, which took over the GWR branch line when Dr. Beeching closed it in 1971, runs steam trains throughout the summer and is an important part of the community transport system and the tourist industry.

The scattered villages and settlements of the parish are linked by lanes, tracks and footpaths. This historical network, once an essential part of working life, has now become an important means of recreation. Where public transport is non-existent, the isolated rural communities are connected with each other through this ancient and increasingly valued facility.

SHORT CUTS

These paths are too short and detached to allow them to be incorporated in the walks but nevertheless are useful to locals and visitors alike. Some of them, notably numbers 4, 7 and 8 pass very close to houses and even pass through gardens. Please stay on the line of the path and keep children and dogs close at hand.

1. BLUE ANCHOR
Between Chapel Cleeve and Blue Anchor, on the RH side, the path follows the edge of Huntingball Wood to join the Watchet road.

2. CLEEVE HILL
From Old Cleeve, 250 yards past the entrance to 'The Double', on the LH side the path leads up the side of a field to the Watchet road.

3. BILBROOK
The path leads from Lower Bilbrook, 50 yards south of the railway bridge over White's Meadow to the A39 at Dragon Cross.

4. LODGE ROCKS
1/4 mile past the turning to Lodge Rocks House the path leads through the garden of Lodge Farm to the road near Thistlewell.

5. WASHFORD
From the railway bridge at Lower Washford, the footpath goes up Cobbler's Steps to join Monks' Path.

6. WASHFORD
Just before the Railway Bridge, on the LH side, the footpath follows the railway embankment behind the houses, turning LH at the end and exiting adjacent to The Washford Inn.

7. ROADWATER
From the centre of the village near the telephone box and opposite the chapel, the path leads up in front of the houses then through the back gardens and fields to join Mount Lane.

8. LEIGHLAND
The path leads through a gate at Mill Reef Farm (opposite Hook Hill) down the sloping field through some scrub and exits onto the track of the Mineral Line.
At the present time it is difficult to follow the track of this path.

One of the aims of this guide was to identify parts of walks or places where less-mobile people could access areas such as a viewpoint or a level walk.

Only a small number of these places have been described, the major difficulty being the type of terrain. Steep hills and rough paths make it difficult for wheelchair users and families with pushchairs.

However, we are fortunate that we have two separate parts of the old Mineral Line as public rights-of-way and recreational use can be made of this historic track.

1. In Washford the Mineral Line runs from the recreation ground to Watchet. It is level, straight and has a sound surface. After about ½ mile, near Bye Farm, there is a gate and stile across the path. If the gate is closed it could prevent further progress. However, the walk even that far is pleasant and easy with the Washford River alongside the path.
   The entrance to the recreation ground is opposite the school at Lower Washford. A sign points to 'Watchet via the Mineral Line'.

2. In Roadwater the Mineral Line is an access road to the houses, ending at Pitt Mill. This road is a public footpath and can be used by all seeking peace and quiet away from fast-moving traffic. Having said that, it is used by a number of vehicles and care must be taken at all times when using it as a footpath.
   The Mineral Line can be reached by turning left in the middle of Roadwater 100 yards past the post office into Station Road (sign – Road ahead narrows to 9 ft.).
   Then turn RH – a sign points to the 'Mineral Line'.

These two walks are suitable for families having children in pushchairs. As an added bonus, both Washford and Roadwater recreation grounds have playground facilities for young children.

North

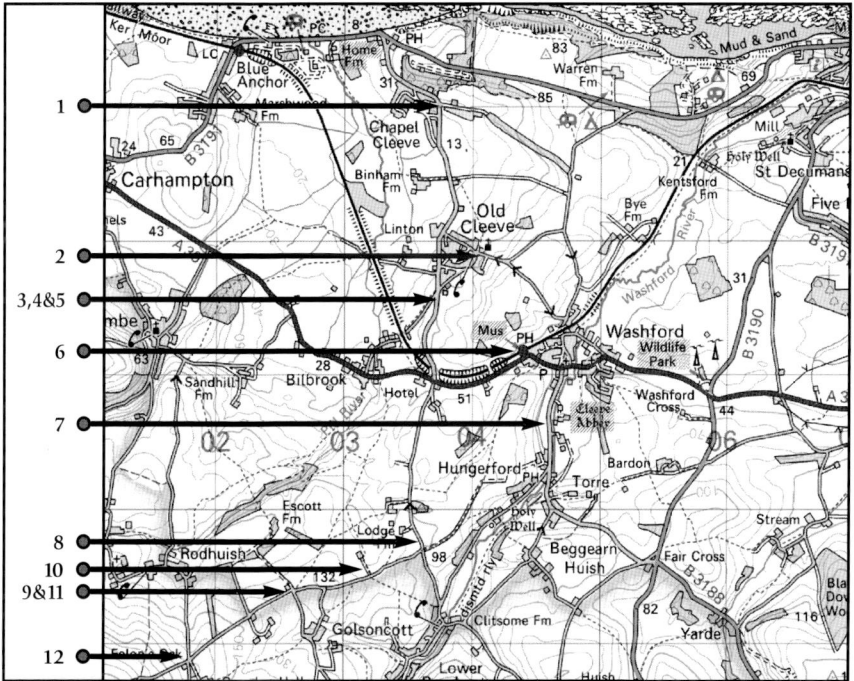

South

Blue Anchor from the cliff path - Walk No. 1

Cleeve Abbey Gatehouse - Walk No. 7

Naked Boy's Stone - Walk No. 23

Bee Orchids from Cleeve Hill

Walk No. 1

Graded : MODERATE
Special features ~ Wild flowers, butterflies and birds

ST 037 430   3¼ miles [5 km]   2 hours
Chapel Cleeve through The Double to Jenny Cridland's Copse.
Kentsford Farm to Warren Bay, cliff path to Blue Anchor,
Huntingball Wood to Chapel Cleeve.
🚌 Follow the road from Old Cleeve towards Blue Anchor.
At the top of the hill in Chapel Cleeve turn RH into Chestnut
Avenue. Park under chestnut trees on LH side.

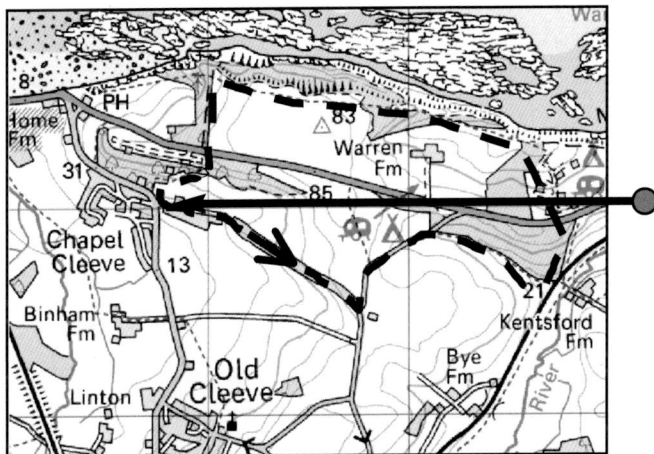

START: Walk along the private road until it divides. Take the LH
fork and follow it almost to the end. Just before it ends at a field
entrance there is a stile and gate on the RH. The permissive path
winds up through the copse and the shady track is well worn
underfoot.
*On either side the earth banks are riddled with holes from a variety of
creatures. There are foxes' earths, badger setts and rabbit warrens all
with different entrances and exits creating an underground maze
hidden from our eyes.*

Keep straight on crossing the farm track. Near the top there is a gateway with a good view of Old Cleeve church and village. Speckled Wood butterflies flit from plant to plant preferring the dappled shade to the sunnier hotspots.

Once over the stile at the end turn LH along the road and walk towards Watchet. After about ½ mile, just round the corner from the bottom of a downhill stretch, the footpath turns RH over a stile.

The area on up the hill and to the LH is known as Jenny Cridland's Copse. No one is sure who Jenny Cridland was but old maps show a dwelling in the fields (once called Oat Erish) but now thick scrub. This piece of land is the most westerly point of Great Britain where nightingales breed. Every year in April, almost to the day (around about the 11th) the nightingales return and from then on until about the end of May you will be almost certain to hear their liquid mellifluous song – not just at night for they sing all day too.

The field opposite the gate sometimes has a grasshopper warbler singing in the margins. They arrive in April and depart in August and you would be lucky to see this shy bird hiding in the grasses.

Over the stile the path leads down through the wood.

There is a selection of trees on the LH amongst which is a stand of the Broad-Leaved Lime, Tilia platyphyllos.

If a squawk disturbs the peace it is likely to be a jay and often the beautiful blue and black striped feathers can be picked up along the path. Long-tailed tits nest in the pine trees - their pink and grey coats and distinctive long tails make them easy to identify.

At the far end of the footpath keeping the railway crossing on the RH, walk on into the field and up the slope. Kentsford Farm is visible on the other side of the railway and the port of Watchet straight ahead.

This whole area, the woods behind and the grassland ahead is a SSSI (Site of Special Scientific Interest). From May through to September the limestone slope is full of wild flowers and therefore butterflies and moths. Many rare species of wild flower grow here, such as Meadow Clary, Salvia verbenaca; Restharrow, Ononis repens; Vervain, Verbena officinalis; Grass Vetchling, Lathyrus nissolia; Flax, Linum bienne, plus some unusual grasses and thistles. Also on this SSSI, not far away from this field, can be found one of Britain's rarest wild flowers, a species brought back from the brink of extinction, the Hairy Mallow, Althaea hirsuta, growing alongside Bee Orchids, Ophrys apifera and Pyramidal Orchids, Anapcamptis pyramidalis.

A visit here from Somerset Rare Plants Group in the spring of 2002 counted 202 different species on this SSSI.

The flowers support a large and varied population of butterflies – on one day in August the following were recorded :

Marbled White, Peacock, Red Admiral, Brown Hairstreak (in the wood), Gatekeeper, Meadow Brown, Brimstone, Clouded Yellow, Common Blue (plus one other very small blue - unidentified), Small Copper, Green-Veined White and Wood White. A great number of fast-flying, non-pitching, small brown butterflies defied identification but added to the fluttering cloud in the summer sun.

Continuing, if you can, (it is difficult to leave this place) walk up the LH side of the field on the footpath to the top gate. Once over the stile great care in needed because of fast traffic. Cross over to face on-coming traffic until you reach **Warren Bay Holiday Site (01984 631460).** *The friendly owners have a camp shop, caravans to rent and a large touring-holiday clientele. They are interested in preserving this part of our coastal flora and fauna and will help if you require information as to the route of the footpath. (1 hour)*

Please keep to the roadway passing down through the caravans to the bottom of the site. The footpath's official track has been rather lost in the site's internal alterations but the most direct way is to bear right into the tenting field and then LH out of it, which takes you to the top of the concrete slipway to the beach. Go down the slipway for a few yards then turn LH at the fingerpost onto the coastal path; the wooded section soon gives way to open fields.

Hereabouts, if you keep your eyes towards the sea, you may well catch sight of one of Britain's larger falcons, the peregrine falcon, soaring overhead and then making a stooping dive from high above.

The field has a footpath leading off to the RH and down to the beach – pass this by and keeping to the RH go over the stile in the corner where you enter the wood again.

From here on, please be aware of the dangerous cliffs ahead. **Children and dogs should be kept close at hand.** *In places the cliff has eroded and the path is only a few feet from the edge. There is little warning of these places of greater risk – suddenly round a corner they appear or they may be hidden in a narrow band of vegetation. There is no danger at all if you keep to the path but youngsters are adventurous and may run on ahead without appreciating that a cliff path has to be treated with caution.*

The cliff path goes on through the wood, a bent tree straddles the path.

Below, safely inaccessible on the grassy vertical slopes, a few specimens of the rare Fly Orchid, Ophrys insectifera, have been relocated growing in the blue/grey marl of the cliff face.

The first field out of the wood has a well-travelled path to follow around the edge, which then leads into a second field.

In the third field, notice the large semi-circular area that has dropped by over 3 feet. This slump is caused by movements in the Jurassic clay and is the first sign of an eventual total subsidence.

Go through the gateway with a good view of Blue Anchor Bay.

This field is a Mesolithic site on which flint and chert implements, including microliths, scrapers and flake knives have been found.

The area of cliff beneath, stretching from Blue Anchor to Lilstock, has special landscape value and is classified as an SSSI owing to the outstanding series of sections through Late Triassic and Early Jurassic rocks, which are of international importance.

The cliffs are locally subject to landslipping and apart from the interesting flora complete examples of fossils can be found in the mudstone and limestone. Remnants of ammonites are scattered along the foreshore and fish fragments together with fish scales, reptile bones and remains can be identified in the bone bed.

Near Blue Anchor there is an area of rock with alabaster deposits. Pink, white and colourless forms of gypsum are found laid out in horizontal layers in the rock face. The rocks and fossils are a unique and unrenewable resource. All those who intend to collect should follow English Nature's 'Code of good practice' and the Code of

Geological Fieldwork operated by the Geologists' Association. An important aspect of responsible collecting is obtaining legal title of ownership of your finds and sharing information with museums.

The stretch of beach containing fossils can be reached from either Warren Bay or from Blue Anchor. In either case it is imperative that you check the state of the tides and only visit on an out-going tide. Tide times are displayed on the Esplanade at Watchet, published in the West Somerset Free Press and given out daily on TV news.

In this area the tide rises swiftly completely covering the beach which may lead to problems as the cliffs are too dangerous to climb.

As you walk on down the field you can catch glimpses of the cliff scenery with the beach far below. Enter the wood at the bottom and follow the path to the point where the sign informs that the path ahead is closed because of cliff falls.

Turn LH on the permissive path and walk up through the wood to the stile onto the main Blue Anchor to Watchet road.

Cross the road into **The Beeches Holiday Park (01984 640391).**
Caravans are available for hire and a camp shop serves the tourists.

Turn LH in front of the house and then after passing two static caravans on the RH turn into a private drive. The drive leads into Huntingball Wood and down past a residence. Please respect the owners' privacy as you walk down their driveway - do not stray off the path. Look to the LH where Old Cleeve can be seen through the trees. After 100 yards turn LH in front of a gate and go down the narrow path to the road. Just before the kissing gate is reached an old wall on the RH marks the boundary of the wood.

On the road a LH turn will return you to Chestnut Avenue.

[Walked in July]

Fossil Ammonite from Blue Anchor
    Arnioceras semicostatum

THE DOUBLE

Walk No. 2

Graded : EASY
Special feature ~ cobbles!

ST 041 419   1¾ miles [3 km]   1¼ hours
Old Cleeve to Chapel Cleeve, on a permissive path 'The Double',
🚌 Begin at Old Cleeve Church lychgate – roadside parking.

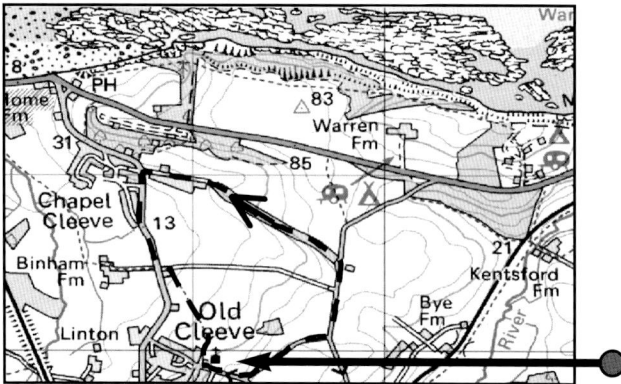

START: Walk up through the churchyard and out onto Monks'
Path, (fingerpost at the top churchyard gate). *The sweet pea on the
bank is the Two-flowered Everlasting-pea, Lathyrus grandiflorus, a
remnant from the garden of a cottage long since demolished.*
*Notice the cobbled drain on the RH side of the road. This connects
with a cobbled causeway at the top of the hill leading to Washford and
which dates from medieval times.*
However, instead of going to Washford, turn LH towards Watchet
at the first signpost. *Badger tracks lead up the hedge on both sides of
the road. A few yards further on the view unfolds – part of the
panorama of West Somerset opens in front of you.*
Continue along the level road. *This is yellowhammer territory, and
in spring, you may also hear the lesser whitethroat singing from the
hedge on your right. Both species have nested here for many years.*
At the next signpost follow the road to the left and after ¼ mile,
pass a farm track (leading to Binham) on the left.

19

Woodpeckers and linnets visit the trees that line the roadside.
Old Cleeve Priory is on the right and has an interesting history.
Formerly New Barn, and noted on the map of 1809, it was purchased
in 1969 by monks of the Community of the Glorious Ascension for
£1000. They lived and worked there until 1980 when the property
was sold to the Alexander Performing Arts Trust for £31,000. In
1987 it became a private dwelling and remains so. There is now a
Woodland Burial Ground on land behind the building.

Just around the corner a stile on the left leads into an open area.
The view from the gateway on a clear day reveals the top of Dunkery
Beacon, at 519 metres the highest point on Exmoor. A notice on the
stile ahead declares this to be a permissive path. The way between
New Barn (now Old Cleeve Priory) and Chapel Cleeve is marked on
the 1809 map as a track. Despite this it does not appear on the
Definitive Map as a right of way although it must have been in use
throughout the 19th century and is recorded as being used throughout
the 20th. In order to regularise the position the Parish Council
applied to the Crown Estate Commissioners for it to be made a right
of way. However, the Commissioners would only agree to it being
designated a 'permissive path' and this was done in 1993.
Speckled Wood butterflies enjoy the shaded woodland from here on.

Climb over the stile into 'The Double'. The path leads
downwards through the wood crossing a cattle track until it
ends in a grassy dell with the sunlight filtering through. The gate
at the end leads into Chestnut Avenue - walk to the end where it
meets the road.

This row of houses was built for the staff of Gerald Stuart Lysaght's
home at Chapel Cleeve. At one time Mr.Lysaght had five chauffeurs
and numbers 1 and 2 lived in the first two houses in the Avenue. The
Chestnut trees, which give the road its name, look unwell but still
provide a good supply of conkers.

Turn left at the end of the Avenue into the road and dodging
cars proceed down the hill. *The chalets of Cleeve Park are well*
screened from the road by some fine oak trees. These are Turkey Oaks,
Quercus cerris, and are identified by their extra long acorns sitting in
big woolly cups.

South Lodge at the bottom of the hill is an early 19th century dwelling. It is listed as being of architectural and historical importance. It was built as the lodge to Chapel Cleeve Manor.

The Manor itself contains remains of a 15th century pilgrim's hospice with ancient connections with the monks of Cleeve Abbey. A succession of three chapels was built at the eastern end of Cleeve Bay (now Blue Anchor), and called St.Mary-by-the-Sea. The first was on the shore circa 1320 and the later ones were built further inland but damaged in 1398 and finally destroyed by landslip in 1452. In 1466 the chapel was rebuilt at the site of the present manor and the statue of the Blessed Virgin Mary, miraculously recovered undamaged from the ruins, installed there.

A hospice / inn was provided near the chapel for pilgrims and fragments of this remain. However, nothing remains of the chapel that gave the hamlet its name.

In time the hospice became a private house, was enlarged in Tudor style in 1818 and 1823 and further enlarged and refronted in 1913-14. It became the home of Gerald Stuart Lysaght who endowed the church and village of Old Cleeve in the first half of the 20th century. Amongst other gifts, the Lysaght Village Hall and Club, the Memorial Cottages, the church clock and one of the bells were generously given for the benefit the village community. After the death of the Lysaghts the manor became a hotel briefly in the late 1950's and the land was sold for housing development during which period the chalet building began. The house has now returned to private ownership.

Continue along the road until you reach Binham Cross; the farm track to the right leads to Binham Farm. If conditions are very wet, you can proceed along the road to Old Cleeve taking first left into the village at the next signpost.

However, at Binham Cross, the best way to return to Old Cleeve is to use the footpath over the field. Turn left beside the house and garage and a stile leads into a field called Church Path and crosses diagonally to the oak tree in the corner - the oak tree has a girth of over 15ft and is at least 300 years old. The farmer leaves a path through the crop to accommodate the right of way but in winter after ploughing you will need sturdy boots.

This is where a great act of vandalism occurred around 1950. Church Path was a cobbled way until the tenant farmer at that time ploughed it into the field and it was lost for ever. You may still see the odd cobble or two buried in the soil but, sadly, that is all that is left of a treasured part of Old Cleeve's heritage.

Pass over the stile and down the steps; more ancient cobbles can be seen here at the bottom – this was the path the monks from Cleeve Abbey used when they walked to the cliff-top chapel. The footpath crosses a wooded track, now unusable, called Port Lane, which in packhorse days would have led up through Rockshill Copse to Watchet. Continue up the steps and along the footpath (rather rough and stony underfoot so care is needed) to the steps at the churchyard's lower gate.

A good way to end the walk is by entering the churchyard and sitting on the seat where you can look over the fields to the sea.

St. Andrew's Church is unlocked from sunrise to sunset and welcomes visitors. There has been a building on this site since well before the founding of Cleeve Abbey in 1198. A small amount of Norman masonry remains but the church was largely rebuilt in 1425 and the tower added in 1533.

Items on sale include a selection of postcards, books and cards.

A free Visitors' Guide notes the interesting features - these include notable stained glass windows, amongst which is a window made and dedicated to commemorate the Millennium, an unusual medieval font-cover, medieval floor tiles made by the monks of Cleeve Abbey and now set around the font, and a cobbled porch.

[Walked in June]

Speckled Wood Butterfly

Walk No. 3

Graded : EASY/MODERATE
(with some wet areas requiring waterproof footwear)
Special features ~ Linton, Marshwood Farm and Binham Farm

ST 037 416   4 miles [6 ¾ km]   2 ¼ hours
Old Cleeve, via Black Monkey, to Marshwood Farm, Blue Anchor
returning via Binham Farm.

From the A39, take the turning to Old Cleeve. Just before the
first signpost to the village, park on the public amenity area
opposite St.Christopher's beside the turning to Bilbrook.

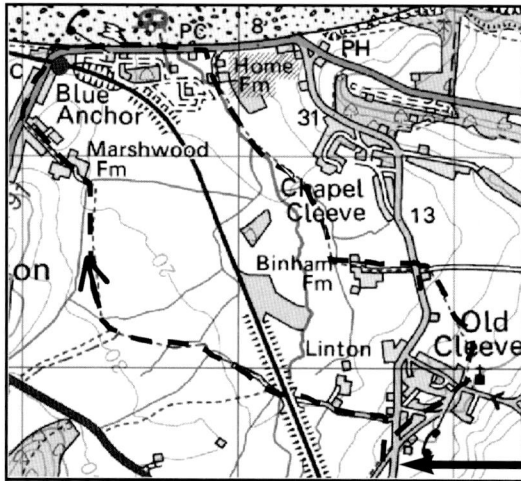

START: Walk down the road towards Blue Anchor for approx.100
yards and take the first turning LH at the signpost to Linton. After
about ¼ mile you arrive at the complex of buildings.
*This was Linton Sheepskin Factory, a tannery established before 1815
but closed in 2001. Hidden behind the old tannery buildings is Linton
farmhouse, first mentioned in records in 1510 and very likely having
some historical connection with Cleeve Abbey. A cobbled path, possibly
part of the network of paths used by the Cistercian monks, ran from Old
Cleeve to Linton and then on to Withycombe, usable in living memory*

but sadly lost in the ploughing and reaping of later generations.

Do not enter the private land ahead, the footpath leads down a stream bed to the LH just before the brick house on the RH. This area is called Black Monkey, a reference to the hooded robes that the monks wore as they passed along these ancient pathways.

The footpath follows the path of the stream overflow, past a large oak tree with a prominent owl box, which successfully breeds a number of Tawny Owls each season.

If you are here in June or July, you may be lucky enough to see a very rare wild flower, Bithynian Vetch, Vicia bithynica, which grows in the hedgerow. You can identify it by the colour of its flowers. Looking like a small sweet pea the bright blue flowers have a conspicuous white standard (the large petal that stands up at the back). Later it produces small, hairy pods.

Above your head the West Somerset Railway passes over Black Monkey Bridge. This fine bridge is a listed building and dates from 1860. It is made of square and coarse punched red sandstone with raking buttresses rising to a parapet with a stone coping.

The path on the RH is raised above the level of the stream bed but is not always negotiable as the hedge becomes overgrown and the bank is eroded. Take to the water, you will have to anyway after you have passed under the bridge. A fingerpost points off to Withycombe parish on the LH but pass this by and walk along the lane. Whatever the season it is muddy, thick squelchy mud usually, but winter walkers sometimes have to ford a veritable torrent.

Watercress, the hybrid form, Rorippa x sterilis, grows in the stream while along the banks aquatic plants such as Meadowsweet, Filipendula ulmaria, thrive. Dragonflies and damselflies, with iridescent coloured wings, flit around over the stream.

After 50 yards the going improves and the path dries out. Big oaks line the fields and the shady path might just hide a shadowy figure dressed in a long black robe......

At one point, where the stream goes off to the LH, cobbles can be seen in the bed of the rocky stream – remains of the Monks' path.

Pass a hunting gate on the RH and keep going down the lane - Marshwood Farm is visible at times over the top of the RH hedge.

A spotted woodpecker taps a message and long-tailed tits, the prettiest of birds, flit from branch to branch and chatter as they go.

Eventually the path takes a turn to the right (the main path continues around leftwards) but it is easy to miss the gap in the hedge just before an electricity pylon. As you turn right into the gap, a field gate appears a few paces ahead under an ash tree, with a stile on the LH. Do not go over the stile – it leads to Withycombe Cross. Instead, go through the RH gate and into the field and then turn LH. After 50 yards go through the field gate.

The sea now appears on the RH horizon with Marshwood Farm at its LH end.

The path follows the edge of the field (officially it crosses the field diagonally but a wide track has always been left by the farmer and it has become an established path).

The land here is beautifully cared for - gates and hedges all in good order - how good to see. Another great joy is to breathe the fresh sea air from the Channel while you listen to the lark trilling as it soars above your head.

A gate leads into the next field and the path continues following the LH hedge until it reaches a further gate leading into Marshwood Farm (the track goes on round the field but is now a farm service track, not a footpath). Through the gate keep straight ahead until you can see the farmhouse.

It is a breathtaking sight, well-tended and hidden from general view. The traditional architecture fits in so well with the surroundings and centuries of use have added to its appeal. The farmhouse rests with its back to the sea, basking in peace and enjoying a panoramic view. Marshwood was Dunster's principal medieval park. In 1428 it covered 270 acres and was valued at double that of the small park at Dunster. In 1755 Henry Fownes Luttrell determined to move the deer from Marshwood to Dunster and this was accomplished at great cost in purchasing land, compensation and fencing. There is in existence a complete specification for the work including "22,720 nails will naile on the pales if none be lost."

Bear right through a gate into the yard in front of the house. Please respect the owners' privacy – the right to use a footpath gives you permission to pass but also a responsibility not to stray or abuse the privilege. Here, I would add, dogs should have been on leads through all the fields but make certain they are on leads in the precincts of the farm where stock come and go throughout the working day - which begins before dawn and ends after dusk! From the house, walk on up through the farm buildings into the lane and onto the track (Tolman Drive) to the main road in Blue Anchor.

Turn RH down the hill to the station. Traffic on the road can be busy and steam trains chuff up and down in the summer - you can collect a train timetable while you are passing if you wish.

Walk along the seafront. In 2002, the western section of the sea wall was renewed and it contrasts sharply with the cracked sections further east. When you cross the River Pill you leave Carhampton parish and return to Old Cleeve parish. A little further on from the Public Conveniences, a RH turn takes you to the **Smugglers Inn**. *Good food can be obtained here and the hours of business and menu are displayed on a board. There is also a function room available.*

Pass round the RH side of the Smugglers and **Home Farm** is ahead. *This is a farm with a prodigious number of diversifications – animals of all shapes and sizes are housed in the outbuildings and this has become a local tourist attraction especially for children as the animals are friendly and provide action-packed hours of fun.*

There is a **Farm Shop (01984 640817)** *specialising in local fresh produce and, best of all, the Teashop provides welcome refreshment and a selection of delicious homemade cakes, or even a tasty "Ploughman's" for the hungry [1½ hrs. excluding refreshments]*

The footpath continues towards Old Cleeve and begins to the left of the teashop passing alongside the hen houses. A stile leads through into the field (called West Cleeve Alders) and initially follows the river. The meadow is swampy and full of rushes, sedges and grasses.

Looking northwards Chapel Cleeve Manor can be seen –
see Walk No. 2 'The Double' for historical information on this building.
A gate leads into the next field - keep following the RH hedge until you arrive at a water tank on a concrete plinth and then go

through the gateway. Here the track of the path becomes obscure, it is supposed to follow the LH hedge but as it is not defined most people follow the RH hedge. However, crop allowing, if you make a bee-line for Binham Farm ahead on the far side of the field you will arrive at a kissing gate which leads onto a concrete trackway. Here fork left, leaving the concrete surface and follow this track which bears right, to pass in front of Binham farmhouse.

Binham was one of the five granges serving Cleeve Abbey. The land passed to the Crown at the surrender of the monks in 1537. The two-storey porch, added in 1624, provides an impressive entrance for the farmhouse and above is the crest, carved in stone, of Robert Boteler. There is a plaster frieze over the porch room fireplace and the whole house remains an imposing residence owned by the Crown Estate Commissioners and let to tenant farmers.

The same advice given at Marshwood Farm applies here - please remember, this is someone's home, and work requirements and farm vehicles have precedence – so keep alert and please exercise great care especially where children are concerned.

Leaving Binham behind, walk along the farm lane to the road. If you turn RH and keep straight on the road will take you back to St. Christopher's after about 1 mile. A more interesting way is to take Church Path leading over the field to the church and village. Opposite the farm drive (this is Binham Cross) go up beside the LH house of the two, and over the stile into the field. Diagonally over the field an oak tree beckons from the corner - a track is left through the crop for the right-of-way. In the far corner, once through the gate, the steps go down and up (cobbled in the middle) and the path leads up a shady passage, which is eroded by water and therefore somewhat rough underfoot, until you come to Old Cleeve Church.

A rest can be taken on the churchyard seat and a visit to the church included (see Walk No. 2 'The Double' for details of history of St. Andrew's). Go past the church and old Post Office into the village. Continue past the **Lysaght Village Hall** where visitors are welcome at the Club during licensing hours when drinks and snacks are available. Keep straight on until you arrive back at St.Christopher's and your parked vehicle.

[Walked in June]

27

Walk No. 4

Graded : MODERATE
Special features ~ Landscape panorama

ST 037 416   3¾ miles [6 km]   2½ hours
Old Cleeve, via Black Monkey, to Crown Wood, Withycombe;
returning to Old Cleeve via Bilbrook.
🚐 On the A39, at Dragon Cross turn in to Old Cleeve.
After ½ mile, park on the LH on verges of the public amenity
area by seats.

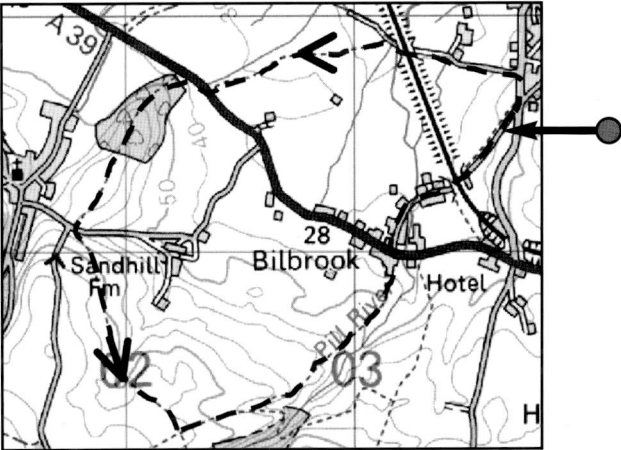

START: Walk down the road towards Blue Anchor for approx
100 yards and take the first turning LH at the signpost to
Linton. *(See Walk No. 3 - Black Monkey, for historical information
about Linton and Black Monkey.)*
The footpath leads to the LH down the bed of the stream, just
before the red brick house on the RH.
*In a dry season there will be little water but usually you will have to
paddle and further down past the bridge, especially in a wet season,
the water may well be over walking boots. The footpath is raised*

above the stream-bed on the RH edge but, despite repair work, it is not always negotiable and you may have to walk in the stream.

Under the railway arch keep to the RH bank passing a fingerpost with an arrow pointing to Withycombe. Just past this is the best place to cross the stream, the bottom has been raised to help walkers cross. Once on the other side the fingerpost points the way through the gate and into the field.

From April to June Yellow Iris (or Yellow Flags), Iris pseudacorus, brighten this shaded passage. The rhizomes (bulbous roots) were once used to produce a black dye and black ink - perhaps the sheepskins at Linton Tannery were originally coloured in this way?

Cross the field to the gate in the diagonal corner.

The field soil is alluvial and very friable – a marked difference from the limestone clag of the higher parts of Old Cleeve.

Once through the gate turn LH and almost immediately go through a gap/gate in the next hedge. Here a narrow sheep path appears to lead over the field straight to a gate – <u>ignore this</u> and instead bear RH to the far corner of the field. Vehicles on the A39 can be heard and Withycombe's Crown Wood can be seen ahead. Go over the stile and follow the RH hedge to the next gate where another stile awaits you. This is where you pass from Old Cleeve parish into Withycombe parish. Climb over this stile and keep straight until you reach the road, aiming for the 40-limit signs ahead, where a stile leads onto the road verges.

Certainly crossing the A39 is a case of 'the quick and the dead'. Assuming the former, and safely on the opposite side of the road, the direction is briefly RH towards Minehead with a short struggle through the verge's long grass bringing you to a gate on the LH.

A fingerpost points to the wood – go through the gate and aim for the far RH end where another gate leads into the trees.

Crown Wood is an ancient, semi-natural woodland, comprised mostly of sessile oak trees. The wood itself dates back at least to 1600 and some of the trees are 250 years old. A statement of policy from the Crown Estate Commissioners reports that it is managed with a minimum intervention/constant cover policy which means that it will not be thinned and never felled.

The footpath leads up the hill and more or less keeps to the wood's RH border although you may have to skirt round obstacles such as fallen boughs and badger setts.

In spring a carpet of bluebells astounds – how ever many times you have seen this natural wonder it cannot fail to gladden the heart. Bluebell woods are amongst the most distinctly British of all plant communities and in the filtered sunshine make an unforgettable picture. These are the native British Bluebell, Hyacinthoides non-scripta, and not, as are becoming more and more frequent, examples of the Spanish Bluebell or the hybrid between the two.

The native bluebell has long tubular bells rather than the round ones of the Spanish and hybrid species. It has graceful sweetly-scented flowers which all droop from one side.

About ten minutes later the footpath emerges from the trees through a gate and into a field, crossing it in a straight line to a gate in the opposite fence. However, you may find an impassable crop, such as maize, barring the way together with a polite and helpful sign from the farmer asking you to divert round the edge of the field. This is entirely reasonable and has the added bonus of providing a fine view of historic Withycombe as you follow the fence round.

The unusual overhead view of Withycombe makes an interesting study with the houses, cottages and gardens laid out below. The 13th century church of St. Nicholas with its lime-washed walls nestles into a cluster of cottages. It has a squat 40 feet high porch tower with small, one-light bell openings and outer door all of about 1250. Inside, of the same date, is a stone effigy of a layman <u>wearing a hat</u> - believed to be the earliest known on a stone monument in England. Alongside the fields and buildings of Court Farm can be identified. It is pleasant to spend a few moments here letting time go by and watching Withycombe at work and play.

When you come out of Crown Wood, if there is no crop to impede you and no resultant small diversion to the RH – you could go and have a look at the view anyway – it is well worth it.

Whichever way you cross the field the footpath exits through the opposite gate, down a grassy path, through another gate and into the lane leading to the road.

Here, just where the lane meets the road, is another reminder of the heritage left by craftsmen of yesteryear. The field on the immediate right is the Glebe field. If you examine the gate into the field you can see that it is no ordinary lash-up of welded pipework or unfinished timber. This is a real gate, fashioned a hundred years ago by Withycombe's village blacksmith, Beadon Case. The gate is as good as the day it was made; each joint is hot-broached and properly finished. It looks as if it will stand for another hundred years. In Withycombe village there are similar gates round the old Rectory.

A fingerpost points the way into the field on the opposite side of the road and here you join the Macmillan Way. The path crosses the field uphill to the opposite hedge where you will find a hunting gate.

The top of the field gives a good view of Sandhill and the now-famous racing stables - usually a number of horses can be seen grazing in the fields below.

With your back to the gate, the path continues in a straight line and roughly at an 11 o'clock angle towards a little wood peeping over the brow of the next field.

Kingsdown Clump sits on the far horizon just left of centre.

At the next gate pass into the small wood which disguises a disused quarry. A minute or so later you come to the gate at the exit and once through this follow the RH hedge up the slope to the top gate by a stony track.

Undo the chain and re-fix, cross the gap still keeping to the RH hedge following it right round the bend. Eventually this leads to a hunting gate and a 'footpath four-cross-way'. In front of the gate the RH path leads to Rodhuish, ahead through the gate is Escott Farm, to the LH is Forche's Lane. Do not go through the gate, but turn LH in front of it and aim for the dip below the far distant BBC masts. *There are some willow trees sinking in a shallow waterlogged depression on the LH side of the field – perhaps this damp hollow is the remains of another long-disused quarry.*

When you reach the hedge a stile reveals itself half hidden in the bushes, and giving access to the next field. Cross this next field in a straight line (you will probably have to 'wade' the crop) heading for a large old oak tree directly ahead. On the oak's left there is a hunting gate marked with direction signs and once through it make for the HT pole on the slope in front. The next stile is under a line of oaks on top of the slope and gives a stunning view in good weather conditions.

Over the stile follow the RH fence down and round the field until you come to a hollow. Down and up the slope of the dip brings you to a fingerpost on the corner.

Looking ahead towards Bilbrook another HT pole can be seen in the near distance – the path crosses the field to the right of the pole meeting the hedge on the bend (a fingerpost leans against the hedge). There is a stile 100 paces further on. Over the stile bear left and upwards, contouring around the slope, and once over the rise you will find another stile. Over this one, follow the fence down to a further stile leading into the precincts of Steps Farm. Immediately opposite the stile there is a gate and this gives way to a path beside the modern house and one further stile leading to the A39 road.

Cross the road into Bilbrook Lane and walk through Lower Bilbrook, along the edge of the ford and back onto the footpath to Old Cleeve at the railway bridge.

Five minutes' walk up the edge of the field returns you to the grass amenity area and your vehicle.

[Walked in April]

BELL SHAPES

Native English Bluebell   *Spanish and Hybrid Bluebell*

Walk No.5

Graded : EASY
Special features ~ well-preserved limekiln & panoramic views

ST 037 416   2 ½ miles [4 km]   1¾ hours
From Old Cleeve to Whitley Brake returning via Steps Farm
🚐 On the A39, at Dragon Cross turn in to Old Cleeve. After ½
mile park on the LH on verges of the public amenity area by seats.
The walk begins at the top of Bilbrook Lane, near St. Christopher's.

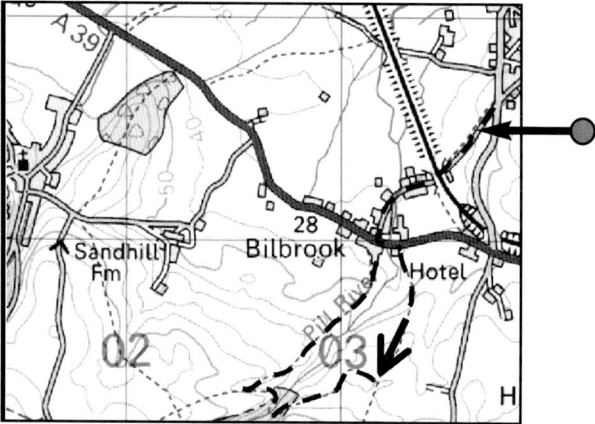

START : Enter the field (Rockleigh) by the sign to Bilbook Lane and
walk down the footpath at the side of the field towards Bilbrook.
After passing through the gate at the railway line onto the road,
keep going past the ford (the second-longest ford in the British
Isles) until you reach the main road where you turn left.
If you stop at the bridge, recently reconstructed, you can see a drain hole
on the LH bank made for the use of otters to try to prevent them crossing
the A39 and inevitable death – the exit drain for the otters is over the
road on the other side of the bridge.
Walk to where the pavement ends and cross the road to Bilbrook
Cottage (fingerpost).

The footpath goes up the track and into the field (called Strinkle Mead) to the left of the house and meanders on round the RH hedge then crosses the field on a track to the left-hand hedge.

At the side of, and ten feet vertically below the footpath, runs Forche's Lane, an ancient packhorse route of which only a part is negotiable. The footpath keeps to the field but if you can find a gap in the hedge it is worth taking a look at this ancient sunken lane, crossed at one point by an unsafe metal bridge.

The views unfold as you journey forwards with eastern Blue Anchor and the Bristol Channel on the RH, then Minehead, and round to Black Hill with its coniferous cap on the far LH.

Keep above Forche's Lane close to the hedge for about ¼ mile and pass through the gateway at the end. The fingerpost points to Golsoncott ahead (this is where Forche's Lane becomes a negotiable footpath all the way to Forche's Garden), however, this walk goes the other way. Take the RH turning to Withycombe and enter the field keeping beside the RH hedge

Growing in the grassland bordering the hedges can be found the Field Scabious, Knautia arvensis. Its sky-blue flowers are pollinated in summer by bees and butterflies - it is one of our most attractive wildflowers.

Follow the curve of the field round for about 100 yards past some large oak and ash trees. Ten yards beyond an electricity pole is a gap in the hedge. Turn right here and enter the rough area of scrub.

There is a single apple tree on your left producing delicious sharp apples in season, with red skins and pink flesh.

There are plenty of opportunities for picnics here, perhaps with apples for dessert!

Further into the copse a specimen ash tree towers on the right and at the end of the wood there is a gate and stile into a meadow. Over the meadow you come into the area known as Whitley Brake.

On the LH side is a limekiln, which used to burn Rodhuish limestone, the kiln being exceptionally well preserved. Just past the kiln, on the left, notice an eroded mud bank, red in colour with one of the layers lighter in colour. This lighter layer is composed of sand laid over the older limestone below – the local name 'Sandhill' being well demonstrated here. On the other side a quarry drops vertically down below the path, unseen because of its wooded covering.

This place is not a great distance from the road but exudes an 'other worldliness' in the sheltered wood.

Proceed down the slope to where the path divides, take the right fork and cross the River Pill.

The River Pill rises above Rodhuish and enters the sea at Blue Anchor - take time to look at the bridge's stone arch under the pathway - it is very well constructed.

In most seasons this is a muddy area and the path is always wet underfoot. Keep the river on your right and if you are quiet you may see squirrels, pigeons and rabbits. Speckled Wood butterflies flit around the brambles enjoying the filtered sunshine and feathers from birds of all kinds can be picked up along the path.

These rural walks require dogs to be kept on leads - through here is a pheasant breeding area so the advice is particularly important as baby pheasants are easily frightened.

Walk up the hill to the gate - go through (or over if necessary) into the next field.

In a previous year the field has grown a crop of sunflowers and a few stragglers still remain.

There is no fingerpost for direction but keeping the large oak on your right, skirt round it and turn sharp right where there is a gate in the hedge. On the other side of the gate, with more lone oaks on the left slope ahead, make for the HT pole in the middle. As you crest the rise you will see the stile beyond.

The nearby oaks have interesting gnarled roots, while in the distance, if you are in a straight line with the stile, is framed the tower of Old Cleeve Church just waiting for a photograph.

The view is your reward for the uphill toil - it is quite literally a 360° view – worth savouring.

Over the stile, follow the RH fence line all the way down the field until you come to a hollow; when you reach it go down the hollow and up the other side to the corner (fingerpost).

Looking ahead towards Bilbrook you can see another HT pole in the near distance in the field; the path traverses the field to the right of the pole, meeting the hedge on the bend (fingerpost). There is a stile 100 paces further on.

Over the stile bear left and upwards, contouring round the slope and once over the rise you will find another stile. Over this one (the top bar is gnawed by the horses) follow the fence down to yet another stile.

There is usually stock in this field, requiring a sensible approach; today there are seven beautiful horses.

The stile leads you straight to a gate (please keep strictly to the path here and do not deviate RH into the farmyard). Pass through the gate and go down the path beside the modern house and over the last stile to the driveway and the A39 road.

A fine and rather unusual tree, a Japanese Walnut, Juglans ailantifolia, graces the area in front of the houses.

On the RH, **Steps Farmhouse (01984 640974)** *provides traditional bed and breakfast accommodation in barn conversions located in secluded gardens. A warm welcome awaits you from Mr. & Mrs. P. James. This side, away from the busy road, the 16th century former farmhouse enjoys a peaceful outlook over the fields, trees and paths of the fringes of Exmoor – a walker's paradise.*

Cross the road into Bilbrook Lane and walk through Lower Bilbrook, along the ford and back onto the footpath at the railway bridge. Only a few minutes walking up the field brings you back to Old Cleeve.

In summer the path is edged with Field Garlic, Allium oleraceum – a pungent plant and one that is becoming less common everywhere.

At the top of Rockleigh you can take a rest on the seat provided by Old Cleeve Women's Institute or, when reaching the road and back on the amenity area, there are two more seats provided for your use. These two seats were erected to commemorate the Queen's Silver Jubilee and give a good view of the Brendon Hills on which you have been walking.

[Walked in July]

Walk No. 6

Graded : MODERATE
Special feature ~ Railway Line

ST 044 412   2³/₄ miles [4¹/₂ km]   2 hours
Washford Station by steam train to Watchet. Return on footpath over Cleeve Hill (or shoreline) to Warren Bay then along the Mineral Line to Washford.
Times of trains on the West Somerset Railway are available at all stations, at Tourist Information Offices or Telephone 01643 707650 for the 24-hour Talking Timetable.
🚌 Turn into Lower Washford off the A39 - coming from Minehead turn LH just after the turning to Cleeve Abbey.
Park along the roadside or turn into Castle Mead where there are spaces for vehicles which do not impinge on the residents' parking. Alternatively you may be able to park in the station car park.

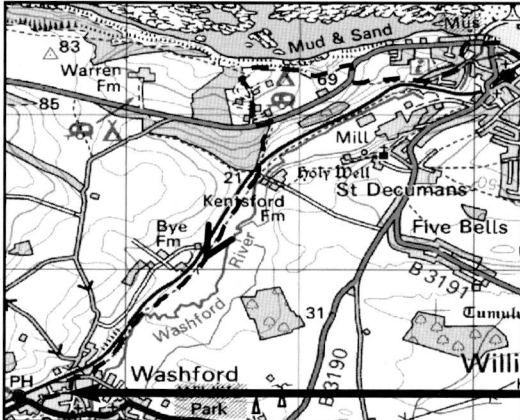

START: Walk through Castle Mead to the A39 road and turn RH to Washford Station. Steam trains run a regular service to Bishops Lydeard and the first stop is Watchet.

The West Somerset Railway was opened in 1870 and the extension from Watchet to Minehead authorised in 1874. It became part of the Great Western Railway until the reign of Dr.Beeching when in 1971 it was closed. Since it reopened as a private enterprise in 1976 it has become a major West Somerset tourist attraction as well as a useful mode of local transport.

Good views can be seen from the windows and after ten minutes Watchet Station is reached. Alight from the train and walk along the platform towards the sea – there is a footpath off this end of the platform going to the Esplanade.

From the Esplanade the new marina can be examined. This was opened in 2001. Also interesting, a little further on, is Watchet's Market House Museum. The Market House was built about 1820 and traders sold their wares through the large windows to folk outside. Don't miss the Court Leet jail round the back. The Museum is open every day from Easter weekend until the end of September.

It has a good collection of local fossils, Stone Age implements, microliths, many photographs of Watchet and the surrounding countryside and displays of the 10th and 11th century Watchet Royal Mint which produced coins for Ethelred, Canute and William the Conqueror. An hour or even two can easily be spent here.

The walk now provides two alternatives, both going to Warren Bay.

    a) Over Cleeve Hill

    b) Along the beach

Alternative a) Continue up Market Lane passing the Old Mineral Yard (on the RH by the telephone box) which was the terminus of the Mineral Line railway.

Over the bridge turn LH and pass beside the Star Inn. The old mill wheel is dated 1879. The river roars as you pass over the footbridge, when you reach the road turn RH - this is Whitehall. After a short distance there is a fingerpost on the RH to Cleeve Hill. This is not the path to take - it only leads out to West Street – so continue along a bit further until you see a sign ahead 'Public Footpath Only'. Follow the RH branch of the lane wending through between the houses until you reach a fingerpost just before the bridge. Take the RH branch to the 'Blue Anchor road'. Go over a stile and into a small field entrance (there may be horses here) and over another stile. Ascend the slope to a stile visible in the top LH corner. Follow the path along the top under the hedge for about 200 yards until you reach the road where a stile leads straight out into the traffic. Turn RH and walk 100 yards back towards Watchet and then into the gateway of the Heritage Field and Dawes Castle on the LH side. Follow the permissive path along the cliff edge of the fields until you reach Warren Bay, turn LH at the concrete ramp * * * *

Alternative b) This is only possible on an **OUT-GOING tide.** It is a 30-minute walk along the shore to Warren Bay.

Times of tides are displayed on the Esplanade at Watchet and given out daily on local radio and television. The sea comes right up to the cliffs at high tide and there is no possible escape upwards because of the dangerous state of the rocks.

ONLY TAKE THIS ROUTE IF YOU ARE SURE IT IS SAFE.

From the museum walk on up Market Street – take a sideways diversion by the side of the Clipper Inn to see the West Pier built in 1869. Return to the street, turning RH and continue into West Street. A little way up a turning to the RH leads down to the beach (just opposite a house called 'Green Gates').

Walk westwards towards Warren Bay, picking your route through pebbles, seaweed and sandy mud, which in places causes your feet to sink a few inches. Maintain a middle track; if you get too close to the cliff you can hear small stones clatter down and you would not want to be underneath. *The rock formations are better viewed from a little distance and can be admired and examined in safety. For a fuller description of the geology of this coastline see Walk No. 1 'Wildlife Walk'.*

Ahead on the cliff you can see Warren Farm, which disappears from view as you round the corner to Warren Bay. Just before the green wooded area reaching down to the beach, there is a gap in the cliff line. The concrete ramp of Warren Bay rises to the Caravan site.

The public footpath actually leaves the beach 100 yards further on but permission has been given for walkers to use the ramp. *As you walk up the slope, above your head on the LH there are some limekilns which were in use until about 1930. Donkeys fitted with*

*panniers carried loads of blue lias stones up to be burned in the kilns
at the cliff top. On Sundays the donkeys were walked to Old Cleeve to
be shoed in the Blacksmith's forge opposite the church.*

* * * * Here the two alternative routes from Watchet combine.
At the top of the ramp turn LH into the camping field and then
RH. Wind your way up and out onto the Watchet to Blue Anchor
road. Turn LH and 150 yards further on a stile (fingerpost) on
the RH gives access to a field. The footpath tracks down the field
to the bottom and leads directly to the railway crossing. Stop,
look and listen and cross the track when all is clear.
Ahead is a four-cross-way (fingerpost). Ahead to Watchet Church
and St. Decuman's holy well; to the left the port of Watchet and
to the right, Washford. The footpath runs along the bed of the
Mineral Railway which brought iron ore from the Brendon Hills
to Watchet.
Turn RH and enjoy the level easy walk back to Washford passing
Bye Farm at about the halfway point.
*Bye Farm was one of the granges of Cleeve Abbey. Situated to the
north-east of the main abbey farm its fields and pastures lay alongside
the Washford River. When the 1838 tithe map was made Bye Farm
was one of the farms subject to tithes. It became part of the Wyndham
Estate but is now privately owned.*
*Bye is now run as an organic farm - good news for the environment.
When the Mineral Line reaches the part where through the trees you
can see the Washford River running alongside, you might glimpse a
blue flash over the water and know that you just missed seeing a
kingfisher!*
The track of the Mineral Line ends just before Washford
recreation ground but the footpath continues on following the
RH hedge round to the entrance gates. Through the gates along
the lane and into the road brings you out opposite Old Cleeve
V.C. Church of England First School. Turn RH up the road past
the school. At the railway bridge turn LH, which will take you
back to the area where you parked your vehicle. If you left your
car at the station, a footpath leads from the bridge through the
houses and ends near the station.

[Walked in August]

Walk No. 7

Graded : EASY
Special Feature ~ A circumnavigation of the abbey site

ST 047 406   3¼ miles [5 km.] 2 hours
Cleeve Abbey to Torre via Trowden Wood and return via Bardon.
🚌 In the centre of Washford, (travelling towards Minehead) take
the LH turning to Cleeve Abbey. The car park for Cleeve Abbey is
on the RH just past the Abbey entrance.

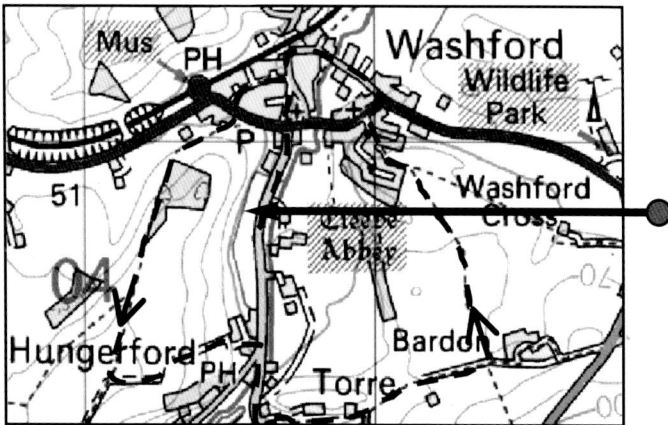

*CLEEVE ABBEY is a scheduled ancient monument and a much
valued and precious part of Old Cleeve parish. In accordance with
this, English Heritage has issued free passes to residents who are now
able to visit and appreciate the beauties of one of the best-preserved
Cistercian monastic sites in the country. Founded in the late 12th
century by William de Roumare, Earl of Lincoln, the cloister buildings
survive, together with wallpaintings, floor tiles and carved timberwork.
The abbey church was destroyed shortly after the Dissolution of the
Monasteries in 1536, but the abbey survived as it was turned into a
private house and was then used as a farm.*

The impressive gatehouse is decorated with a square panel carved with the name of the last abbot, William Dovell, and welcomes visitors through its portals today as, by tradition, it must have welcomed and succoured them in past centuries.

Cleeve Abbey (01984 640377), *has an excellent gift shop and is open from 10 a.m. to 4 p.m.(winter) and 10 a.m. to 6 p.m. (summer).*
START: After your visit to the Abbey, turn RH towards Washford and walk along past Washford Mill to the A39.

Should you need provisions, **Washford Post Office (01984 640349)** *is over the road opposite St. Mary's Church, and has well-stocked shelves for grocery requirements – bread, milk and many other commodities. One of only two post offices left in the parish the proprietors would be happy to direct you if you need help.*

A safe diversion has been made around the back of Washford to avoid the extremely narrow and busy section of road up to the garage 100 yards to the left. Do not be tempted to take the short cut - instead, walk towards Williton, then turn immediately LH. Pass Willow Grove on the RH, (or, if you visited the shop, continue up past the shop) then LH into Castle Mead. At the far end of Castle Mead the footpath exits onto the pavement opposite the garage.

Turn LH along the pavement and cross the road to the garage where a fingerpost is visible at the far end. Pointing behind the garage it leads into the field. Two adjacent signs 'Rams – collisions inevitable' and 'Bull in field' might make the nervous contemplate retreat but press on over the stile and keep to the LH hedge – if there is livestock in a field with a footpath, it should be quite safe to go through.

Follow the ragged fence along the LH edge, pass through a gap and continue along this line until you reach the corner of Trowden Wood where a stile leads into the next field.

Trowden Wood is an ancient woodland of mostly mature oak trees with an underplanting of hazel providing nuts for the squirrels.

The path continues up the hill close to the wood on the LH reaching another stile almost at the end of the wood. In the next field the view opens out to include Bilbrook and Black Hill and a clear view towards Minehead. It is sobering to think that the valley below was one of the projected routes for the now-shelved local bypass.

Continue along the line of the hedge to the ladder stile in the bank at the end of the field. This leads into the next field where the path becomes a track. Walk along this until a large gap in the LH hedge reveals a further track leading away to the left. This is a diversion from the line of the definitive footpath. This track leads down to Hungerford Farm and Torre and is used with the farmer's consent having been a bridlepath for many years.

A footpath marked on the map, further on towards Lodge Lane, which went to down through the wood on the LH meeting the road at St.Pancras is no longer usable. It is hoped that work to reinstate it will be undertaken in the future.

Follow the track around to the left and then immediately right in an S-bend and down the slope towards the farm. The track goes LH through the barns, RH in front of the house and so to the road.

This farm, now Hungerford Farm but historically called Stout's Farm, was one of the five granges belonging to Cleeve Abbey. It farmed the land around the abbey in what was originally called Vallis Florida or Flowering Valley. A medieval park used for hunting was established at Stout around 1507.

Hungerford Farm (01984 640285) *offers Bed and Breakfast accommodation in a traditional farmhouse having, amongst other features, a Tudor grate and fireplace dated 1550-60.*

The farm still manages the land surrounding the Abbey site as it has done for centuries.

Opposite Hungerford Farm, the **White Horse Inn (01984 640415)** *provides an opportunity for refreshment during licensing hours.*
Pub meals are available (outside in the good weather).

Those who are short of time could walk down the road to the LH which leads back to Cleeve Abbey – but the walk continues around the perimeter of the abbey by turning RH signposted Monksilver. Walk up the road, with the river on your RH, past the Trout Farm and over what was a part of the old Mineral Line. Round the corner, just after Torre End House the fingerpost points to the LH and the path leads up between some old stone walls. A little way up leave the main track, following the posted diversion to the RH along the grassy path through the trees.

A family of long-tailed tits chatter above in the trees and patches of Green Alkanet fringe the path with their bright blue flowers.

Leaving the woodland behind you come to an area of bracken which borders on a commercial site of part vehicle tip and part cement works. However, this is soon left behind as a 3-bar stile leads out into open fields and nature reasserts herself. A different view of Cleeve Abbey is outlined behind as you follow the line of oaks on the RH to a gate ahead. There are no footpath signs this side of the gate but they are visible on the other side – this is now part of the Macmillan Way.

Over the gate the lane passes through what was once an entrance marked by the remains of two stone pillars. These were at one time part of the estate gates to Bardon Manor and indicate its importance in times past. The lane is enclosed by trees and lined with wild flowers – a quiet mysterious place. It can be very wet after rain with giant puddles to negotiate. An official temporary diversion into the fields to avoid the waterlogged lane is optional.

Gaps in the RH hedge permit windows into the fields and these are also full of wild flowers – a white carpet of Scented Mayweed, Matricaria recutita, intermingles with Field Pansy, Viola arvensis, while the field awaits the winter plough.

At the end of the lane, turn LH just before the first building, and enter the field. Walk up the field edge on the narrow border joining a track where the hedge ends and leaving the field through the LH of two gaps in the hedge ahead. Those with O/S maps will see that the footpath is marked as going down the other side of the hedge. This was the official line but general usage over a number of years has dictated that the footpath follows this side of the hedge round to the gate and this route has now become established. Walk along the RH field edge and then right round to the kissing gate in the far corner. The tree-covered depression in the middle conceals a pond.

In October, this field was full of wild flowers - Shepherd's Purse, Wild Radish, and Field Pansy all combined underfoot to make a sweet-scented floral mosaic.

Through the kissing gate, walk down beside the houses and into Belle Vue, turn RH which leads to the A39. Once again at the main road, the dilemma, which Washford people daily endure, faces you. Cleeve Abbey lies to the left but a treacherous piece of road prevents safe conduct. So, cross the road, and a quick run in the other direction will bring you to Walnut Tree Corner. (The old walnut tree on the bank recently died and has been replaced with a young one.)

Walk down Huish Lane towards the school and just before you reach it turn LH into the little lane, called McKinley Terrace. Follow this round to the LH and then RH and through the sheltered housing units of Willow Grove – this is still the official footpath – keep on the track that has cobbles in the middle and then at the Community Centre turn RH out to the road which leads to the A39.

Cross the A39, and join Abbey Road leading back to Cleeve Abbey car park. Before you arrive there, **Washford Mill (01984 640412)** *on the RH, as well as Badcock and Evered's farm products and animal feed supplies, has many different retail units including a variety of craft and gift shops, a food store, country clothing, a plant house, and an Alternative Treatment Centre. A very pleasant restaurant, the Miller's Kitchen, provides excellent snacks or meals. Badcock and Evered open every day from 9 a.m. to 5 p.m. and on Sunday from 10 a.m. to 4 p.m. The retail units open every day from 10 a.m. to 5 p.m. and Sunday from 10 a.m. to 4 p.m.*

[Walked in October]

Field Pansy
Viola arvensis

LODGE ROCKS

Walk No. 8

Graded : EASY
Special feature ~ Pastoral landscape, fields and lanes.

ST 036 397   2½ miles [4 km]   1¼ hours
From Lodge Rocks round the fields to Thistlewell. Down to
Roadwater, returning up Batallers Lane.

🚌 From Dragon Cross take the turning to Roadwater up Lodge
Rocks. Stop at the first signpost – this is called locally, Piano
Corner. Park at the roadside without blocking field entrances.

* * There is a problem concerning part of this footpath. It is hoped it
will be resolved in the short term but at the time of printing this guide
an alternative is required. Directions for this diversion are printed in
the text at the appropriate place.*

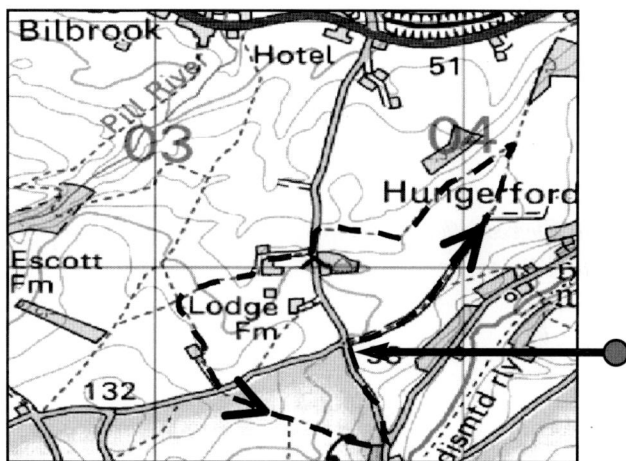

START: This walk begins at the hunting gate on the LH and
passes along a track, walking towards Trowden Wood and
Washford for a distance of about ½ mile. The small gate is wide
enough for a wheelchair or a pushchair.

The footpath along the field is level and firm. Those who use wheelchairs and families with children in pushchairs may find it possible to use part of this track. Good views and peaceful surroundings are found here.

A little way along the track you pass an old barn, shrouded with nettles and willows.

This is usually a good place to find wild flowers. In late summer, Betony, Stachys officinalis, which is one of our rarer plants, can be seen along the grass verges here, as can St. John's-wort, Hypericum perforatum. In the early summer the field edges occasionally hide an orchid or two - there is always something to see.

Follow the track past a line of old oaks on the LH, then past a footpath going RH at a gate (marked on the O.S. map but at this point unusable due to erosion) and finally, also on the RH a little further on, a track going down to Hungerford Farm.

The main track ends at the next hedge – at this point wheelchairs and pushchairs would be unable to proceed.

Here the footpath turns back and crosses the middle of the field you have just walked along – aim for the middle of two HT poles – Halscombe Wood is below on your RH. Pass through the gap in the hedge.

The hedges of these fields are laden with juicy blackberries, which seem to be larger than the normal ones - a sweet treat!

Follow the LH hedge in the next field and pass through another gap into the last field before the road and walk down the RH side where a headland has been left (a headland is a strip of land left uncut and uncultivated around the perimeter of a field).

Broad Pit, a little circle of trees with a small pond hidden in the canopy lies away to the RH.

47

The footpath goes straight to the gate but, taking due consideration for any crop, walk the little extra distance round the edge if necessary.

These small fields are left as they have been for many generations. Sheep and horses co-exist in friendly harmony, the hedges are left intact, long grass proliferates at the edges and the attendant wildlife thrives. Numerous ladybirds were on the rampage causing the greenfly to be under attack during a sunny September. When the grass is parted, beetles and hoppers of all description can be seen hiding amongst the stems.

Once in the road, called Lodge Rocks, turn LH and walk gently uphill for about 100 yds to an entrance on the RH. The footpath turns in between the copper beeches lining the avenue to Lodge Rocks House.

* If there is no fingerpost here, do not turn into the drive – it will be necessary to miss out this section until further notice. Keep on the road, passing Lodge Rocks Cottage on the LH, and a little further on a track leading away on the RH to Lodge Farm. When you reach Piano Corner turn RH. Walk up the road passing Gracepits Copse (with a hidden pond), until you see Thistlewell on the LH. Just opposite the entrance the fingerpost points into the RH field.

* If the fingerpost points the way to the Lodge Rocks House you can assume the footpath is open. Walk down between the avenue of copper beeches and follow the direction signs through the site and into the field.

Cross the field in a diagonal line. At the hedge the footpath joins Forche's Lane. (If you have an O.S. map, note that the footpath is shown crossing in a straight line. This is no longer correct. The original access through the hedge has long gone and the path now goes to the RH corner.) Once over the stile turn LH for about 25 yds. then go over another stile. Walk along the edge of the field, over a stile sheltering under an ash tree, and into the next field. Continue to the end of this field where a barn on the RH marks the beginning of Thistlewell and just past it on the LH a stile in the hedge leads into the farm track.

The footpath passes directly in front of the farmhouse and it is important not to stray off the marked route when on a public right-of-way adjacent to private property, particularly if it is a working farm such as this.

Walk to the road through the line of poplar trees.

These are mostly the Black Poplar, Populus nigra, with the exception of two at the end near the road which are hybrids, Populus x canadensis. The effect of the avenue is stunning and pleases the eye even though the trees are not yet mature.

* * This is the point where the temporary diversion joins the walk. Cross the road and go through the LH of the two gates into the field taking a middle direction downwards to a gap in the hedge. 'Macmillan Way' appears on direction signs. Go down the field edge to the bottom where the path slips sideways into a lane. Go over a stile (houses below) and, right at the bottom, down the steps into Batallers Lane.

(The unusual name is possibly a derivation of 'alders').

Turn LH and walk up the lane between the high banks.

The rich red till shows clearly the conglomeration of rounded pebbles indicating the stones were washed and formed in a riverbed during some former geological age.

About ten minutes walk will bring you back to Piano Corner.

[Walked in September]

Bramble
Blackberry
Rubus fruticosus

Walk No. 9

Graded : EASY
Special features ~ Packhorse route and remains of ancient leat
(A leat is a trench for transporting water to a mill)

ST 026 394   2¼ miles [3½ km]   1½ hours
From Forche's Garden to Escott Farm, returning up Forche's Lane.
🚌 From Dragon Cross, take the turning to Roadwater and turn
right at the first signpost (Rodhuish 1 and Croydon Hall). Pass
one LH signpost to Golsoncott and at the second signpost, 1.6
miles from Dragon Cross, there is a cottage called 'Forche's
Garden'. Turn RH up the lane. About 25 yards in, park in the
open area under the hedge, being careful not to obstruct the
tracks or gateways.

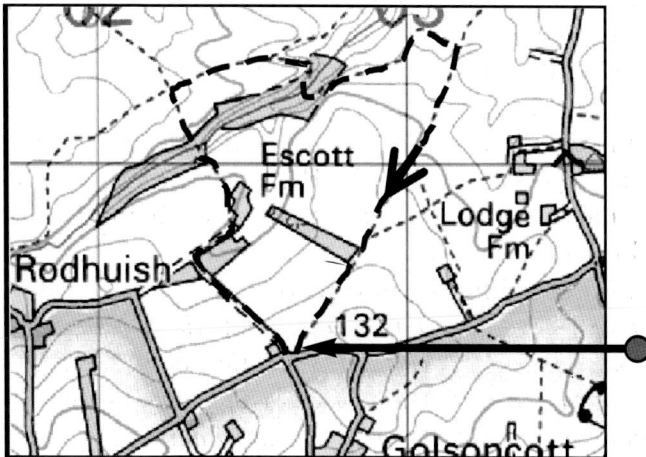

START: Facing the cottage, Forche's Garden, go through the field
gate immediately on the RH (arrow on gate post) then on down
the farm track which leads to Escott Farm. There are signs here
for the Macmillan Way, a long-distance walk, which also passes
along this track. Go through a spinney and over a cattle grid.
If you hear ducks or frogs there is a big pond in the private grounds on

50

the RH obscured by trees. Escott Farm, a private residence, is ahead, just inside Withycombe parish, hidden away from other habitations. The traditional mullioned windows date from 1630 - the Georgian front of the farmhouse being a later addition. There is an unusual plaster porch lined with shells and a path has the date 1735 marked on it.

Keep the farm on your RH, continue in a gentle LH curve along the track past the farm buildings until you start to descend through some shale banks. Follow the main track – there are other tracks serving the farm fields but the footpath goes straight down to the Pill River. Near the bottom a post and sign point the direction ahead so keeping on the track cross the river and continue upwards, exiting the wood at the next fingerpost. Leave the track and walk straight over the field through the middle. There may or may not be a path left for this. If there is a standing crop and no path you can skirt round the RH field edge to avoid crop damage. Whichever way you choose, the footpath leaves the field through a small hunting gate in the hedge in the opposite corner from your entry point. (You cannot see it until you are halfway over the field.) At this gate four footpaths meet. Once through the gate turn RH and follow the hedgeline where there is a wide margin round the edge to accommodate walkers (the official path crosses the field). The stile is reached along the second side of the field - it is almost invisible until you reach it as it is buried in the greenery.

Go over the stile into the next field.

Note the red, sandy soil and the differing variety of crops grown on this farm. Today, in August, 2002, it is a variety of an Asian grass, Miscanthus sacchariflorus, a 'biomass' crop grown to provide fuel for power stations. The farmer has also planted among his crop a distinctive and rather striking mauve weed, Phacelia tanacetifolia. This is to encourage bees and therefore pollination.

Cross the field in a straight line to the large oak tree on the opposite side where the track forks. Take the RH fork, go through (or over) the gate and down the slope. The advice at the beginning of this book regarding dogs on leads must be adhered to here please – although you may not see them this is a pheasant breeding area and it would be insensitive to allow dogs to disturb the pheasants and chicks which are a 'crop' and part of the farmer's livelihood.

At the bottom of the muddy path, cross the river and make your way up the hill to the left.

Before you reach the limekiln on the RH, look down the LH slope. Some 10 feet down can be seen the path of a channel or leat which watered the meadows further down. You can trace the track of the leat right round the slope. After you cross the meadow, look down on the LH while you climb the stile and the leat's ditch can still be seen although it has not been used for many generations.

There are moves afoot to restore this ancient waterway together with the bridge over the Pill River and the limekiln in order that these rural treasures may be saved as part of our historical and agricultural heritage.

Once over the stile go through the coppice and scrub and turn LH at the hedge gap.

Walk round the field until you reach a point where three fields meet. At the fingerpost take the RH fork into Forche's Lane.

Forche's Lane is an ancient trackway, running from Bilbrook to Golsoncott. Various suggestions have been made as to the derivation of Forche - some suggest that the lane was used to take the sheep stealers to Felon's Oak to be hanged, and in French: 'forçat' is a convict condemned and latin 'furcas' is a gallows. No doubt it was the last walk for some, but it must have been an important route in its time directly connecting Old Cleeve with Croydon and the Brendon Hills. Sometime, possibly during the latter part of the 19th Century, the bottom piece of Forche's Lane fell into disuse. The Definitive Footpath Map of 1904 shows the track of the footpath running along the field edges above the sunken lane – as it does today.

However, the top part of Forche's Lane on this walk is negotiable and once on the track you can imagine those pilgrims of long ago, with laden packhorses wending their way upwards towards the ancient settlements of Golsoncott and Croydon.

The track is wide and the going is good except for one part where it is usually wet underfoot and small diversions have been made to accommodate this difficulty. Generally, keep on straight, dipping under a large fallen tree and then over a stile. Another stile leads into a field margin and at the end of the hedge you can see the opening in the RH field and another stile ahead. Over this stile you return to the continuation of Forche's Lane.

The trees lining the lane's banks include hazel, a species much favoured by dormice. Nuts from the hazel bushes here have been positively identified as having been opened by dormice - the hole in the nut has a smooth inner rim. The dormouse, Muscardinus avellanarius, is a small mammal which spends three-quarters of the year 'asleep', hibernating from October to April or May. As an endangered species, dormice are protected by law, and so is their habitat. The loss of the latter is one of the reasons for their decline.

This secretive mammal is easily recognised (should you be so lucky) by its thick furry tail, bright golden-brown colour and bulging black eyes. A late evening in the summer is the best time for a sighting.

In early spring primroses and violets colour the banks of the lane and later it is frothy white with the flowers of the garlic, Ramsons, Allium ursinum.
Continuing on the walk, eventually after about 1/2 mile of a peaceful gentle uphill journey, you leave the wooded banks of Forche's Lane, emerge into daylight and out onto a wide grassy track.

100 yards further on the car is parked beside Forche's Garden.

(Walked in August)

Dormouse
Muscardinus
avellanarius

Walk No. 10

Graded : EASY
Special feature ~ Golsoncott's New Barn

ST 033 395   1½ miles   [2¼ km]   1 hour
From Thistlewell via Golsoncott to Roadwater Farm and return.
🚌 From Dragon Cross take the turning to Roadwater and turn
right at the first signpost – signed to Croydon Hall. (This corner
is locally named 'Piano Corner' after a piano fell off a lorry 50
years ago during transportation to Croydon and was scattered
along the roadside.)
After ¼ mile there is a farm entrance to Thistlewell, the drive
neatly lined with an avenue of Poplar trees. Immediately
opposite this entrance there are two field gates with room to park
between. The road is narrow and the wider bits are for passing
places so please do not obstruct these if the above parking space
is in use. Rather, return to Piano Corner where there is room for
a car or two.

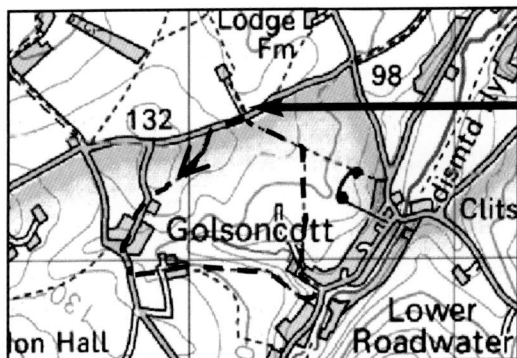

START: Walk 250 yards up the hill from the modern farmhouse,
which is called Thistlewell. Just opposite an oak tree the
fingerpost points LH into a field the name of which is 'Great
Hill'. This is arable land and more than likely a crop will be
growing with no visible path through, although the footpath

actually crosses the field diagonally to the right. Make your way in that direction, straight over using the tractor lines as a path, around the RH hedge or down the LH one. The footpath leaves the field ¾ of the way down the opposite hedge and exits through a gap and down into the road. Walk on until you reach Golsoncott village at Higher Golsoncott Farm.

The old walls sprout colourful pockets of Red Valerian, Centranthus ruber, which although a Mediterranean species, is locally common and naturalised on walls throughout West Somerset.

Continue through the settlement as the road curves round. A stream appears on your LH and after passing some houses converted from barns the road arrives at a junction. Take the LH fork at Escott Cottage, the signpost indicating Roadwater.

200 metres on the LH, after the last house, a fingerpost points into the field. The footpath crosses the field in a straight line towards the farm buildings visible beyond the tall Douglas Fir trees.

Another stile at the far end opens out on to a track and another little path goes down to the LH.

A Monkey Puzzle Tree or Chile Pine, Araucaria araucaria, has been planted at the edge of the path and looks very happy. The seeds used to be eaten as dessert nuts in South America, and Archibald Menzies first brought the tree into cultivation in the late 1790's by slipping some nuts from a Chilean banquet into his pocket.

Keep straight on - New Barn is ahead, the footpath going right through the farmyard.

The old barn down on the LH is called New Barn, and is in fact a very ancient building. Indeed, records of settlements at Golsoncott date from 1221 with the land being then in the ownership of Cleeve Abbey. At the dissolution in 1536 rent from Golsyncoote is listed as £4 11s 10d. Apart from Old Golsoncot Farm, which is believed to have been a fortified manor house, these are the oldest buildings in Golsoncott. The barn, originally a thatched cottage, suffered a dire fate in 1953 when it was partially demolished by the farmer/owner who removed the roof and top storey and turned into a cart-shed.

Walk through the farmyard to the end and then through the gate into the field. The footpath runs round the LH edge of the field and after about 200 yards you come to a gate. Go through the gate and straight over the field to the opposite hedge where you will find a new stile. The footpath goes down the LH side of the field to Roadwater Farm. However, the horses which graze here have been known to be rather 'friendly' so the thoughtful owner has fenced the edge of the field. If you are at all worried turn sharp left at the gate and keep behind the fence on the sloping edge of the field all the way down to the bottom gate just past a huge oak tree.

The river chortles below as you proceed downwards and numerous hedge sparrows rustle through the branches of the hazel and ash trees. A yaffle, or green woodpecker, squawks from the scrub and flies off flapping through the air.

Once in the lane you can spend a few moments admiring the trees, particularly a Cedar of Lebanon, Cedrus libani, in the garden of Roadwater Farm. Roadwater Farm was originally built as a private house to replace the old farmhouse, which in turn became farm cottages and finally farm buildings.

Turn LH, passing Leat House, following the public footpath. The leat runs down a channel on the RH side. Bear RH and immediately in the wall on the LH side of the haybarn a small gate with a 'Public Footpath' sign shows the direction ahead. Go into the little meadow, which is full of buttercups and clover as wells as purple heads of Selfheal, Prunella vulgaris.

Continue upwards, more or less in the middle, pass through a gap and then immediately follow the RH hedge onwards and upwards. Go through another gap into a field and follow the RH fence to the opposite hedge - there are often horses in these fields. A stile takes you into the next field where the path follows the LH hedge eventually arriving at a gate. The footpath now turns LH through a gap and leaves the edge of the field crossing over the middle towards the electricity poles in the skyline opposite (walk in a midline direction).

At the far end a stile leads back into the road at Thistlewell.

[Walked in October]

Walk No. 11

Graded : MODERATE
Special feature ~ Croydon, site of a Cleeve Abbey Grange

ST 026 394   3 miles [5 km]   2 hours
Golsoncott to Roadwater returning to Forche's Garden via
Croydon
🚐 From Dragon Cross take the turning to Roadwater and turn
RH at the first signpost. Pass one LH signpost to Golsoncott and
at the second, 1½ miles from Dragon Cross, there is a cottage
called Forche's Garden. Turn RH up the lane.
About 25 yards in, park in the open area under the hedge. There
is room for two vehicles without obstructing gateways.

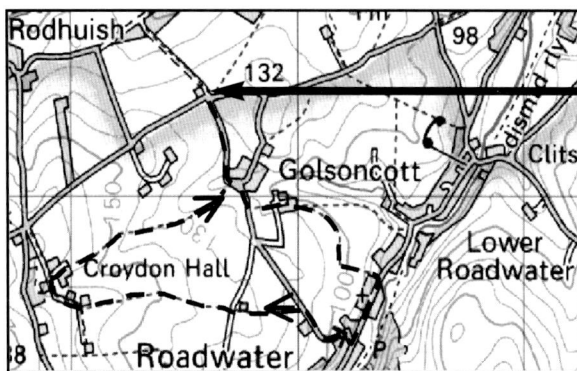

START: Walk back to the road.
Forche's Garden is one of the estate cottages originally belonging to the
Reckitt family of Golsoncott House. They were Quakers and famous for
Reckitt's Blue and Reckitt & Colman Mustard. Their daughter, Rachel
(1908 - 1995), was an artist of international renown, who was also
skilled in sculpture, iron and metal work. Local examples of Rachel
Reckitt's unique work can be found in Old Cleeve Church, where in
1972 she designed and made a screen, and also in Rodhuish and
Withycombe churches. Other works included inn signs at

Roadwater's Valiant Soldier and the White Horse at Torre - this one is now preserved in the inn's skittle alley.

A choice of directions here – either go straight down the road to Golsoncott, after 5 minutes you will arrive at Escott Cottage *(see below). Or, more interestingly, turn LH and walk up the road. After 5 minutes you reach a signpost to Golsoncott (passed on the way).

In spring and summer it is likely that larks will be singing in the fields on either side but today, a cold buzzard perches on the post, fluffs its feathers and looks us straight in the eye.

Turn RH to Golsoncott, reached after another 5 minutes. It lies at the bottom of the hill with Higher Golsoncott Farm on the RH.

Note the stone mounting post (it appears to be an old gatepost) under the beech tree on the right. No doubt Miss Rachel Reckitt from Golsoncott House would have used mounting stones such as this as she travelled round her estate by horse. Even in the latter part of the 20th century she would often be seen in the lanes riding sidesaddle. Good balance and horsemanship were required to keep one's seat and still look elegant, all of which she managed with the same skill she brought to her artistic career.

Old Golsoncott Farm on the LH is believed to have been a fortified manor house. The original house, which was possibly Saxon, lies behind the more recent addition and is a listed building.

Continue on the road turning LH at Escott Cottage (signposted to Roadwater) and the point where the quicker route joins. *

Where the hill levels out there is a fingerpost and stile on the left. Enter the field and cross to the opposite hedge aiming for the left of some large conifers (Douglas Fir) where a stile (yellow waymark) gives access to a path and then joins a track. The footpath leads straight ahead and through to New Barn which lies a little below on the left (see Walk No. 10 – Golsoncott, for historical details). Walk through the farm buildings and then through the gate into the field. Follow the hedge round on the LH side until another gate appears. Through this, turn immediately right and follow the hedge along until a rather superior stile is reached – this has a dog creep post. It has, however, no fingerpost and no directions and it can be a confusing point.

Hedge Hedge Stile Hedge

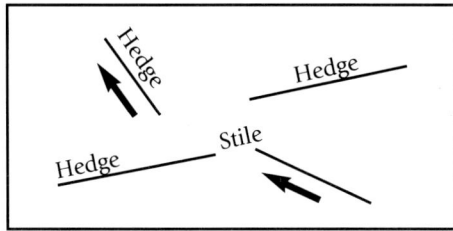

Pass along the hedge as the diagram above shows.

At the end of the hedge there is a wide opening - a disused stile disintegrates on the LH. In the middle of the field on the right a lone ash tree signals the existence of an historical hedge, now long gone. Pass through the gap, turn LH going down the hedge to the trees.

Another stile leads into the wood and as you descend sounds of the Washford River can be clearly heard below. There are some good specimens of Douglas Fir and some tall Pines in the wood. The path goes down quite steeply and exposed roots set a trap for the unwary.

Through the trees on the left you can see the **Singer Instrument Factory.** *Almost at the bottom, an unusual tree towers over the path (the last tall tree on the LH). Its name is Tree of Heaven, Ailanthus altissima, and it is native to mountain woods in China. High above, its leaves are up to a metre long and have 15 (or more) pointed leaflets - none in winter but a beautiful sight in summer).*

At the bottom, between the houses, the path end in Roadwater.

Turn RH, walking past Roadwater Church - this was a Mission Church built in 1876 of sandstone from Lodge Rocks quarry and given by Mrs. G. F. Luttrell, for a total cost of £350. Until the early part of the 20th century the church was used as a school during the week, the altar being screened off by a curtain. Above the door is a bell turret and inside on the LH is the church room. The church is simply adorned, with a high, pitched roof. It has a stained glass window above the altar and an unusual font with a metal liner. It will be open and is worth a visit, and may provide a welcome rest. Continue along the road to the Recreation Ground on the LH.

The land for this, called Day's Meadow, was given to Roadwater by Captain Bridges of Croydon Hall and inaugurated in 1926.

The Village Hall was given by Mr & Mrs Norman Reckitt of Golsoncott House in 1928. It was designed in the style of a farm building by the same Mr. Reckitt, an architect, using local stone.

Just past the village hall, **Roadwater Village Stores and Post Office (01984 640296)** *occupy the previous garage site on the left and have all the usual provisions, including newspapers, bread, milk, ice-creams, chocolate and drinks plus some surprising extras.*

This is one of only two post offices in the parish, both of which provide a vital service to residents.

Mount Lane is opposite the village hall. Signpost : Golsoncott. A short distance (5 minutes) up the rather steep lane, pass one gate on the LH with a fingerpost pointing to the footpath (a short cut) leading back down to Roadwater.

In the trees which line the field two Great Spotted Woodpeckers perch in the treetops with their red markings showing clearly in the leafless branches. Warming their feathers in the winter sunshine they suddenly veer off in an undulating flight towards the next copse.

At the second gate on the LH, after the two barns, the footpath on the LH leads off into a field (fingerpost).

Follow the RH hedge to the far end - the view on the LH is of Leighland. The gateway that leads out of the field enters Blindwell Lane; the footpath crosses the lane and leads into a field on the RH. (The fingerpost and stile are partially hidden opposite, round the corner.) Once over the stile follow the LH hedge through two fields.

In winter, ice patterns the rich red furrows. Covering the path, paper-thin glassy sheets crackle as you crunch through them.

At the end of the second field before you reach the field gate a smaller gate leads off left.

Ahead is Croydon and in summer this last field will be garnished with wild flowers or 'weeds'– Common Field-speedwell, Veronica persica, and Field Madder, Sherardia arvensis, amongst others.

A hedge, mostly of holly, forms the field boundary right up to Home Cottage with a stile at the far end. In the lane keep straight ahead, passing Croydon Hall on your RH.

Croydon was one of the five granges held by Cleeve Abbey in the 16th century. Close to the western boundary of the parish it is recorded as being let in 1517 to George Prowse; it consisted of 172 acres of land and 12 acres of wood. The annual rent to the abbey was £4.17s, together with the promise that each year the tenants would provide dinner and supper for the abbot and 20 men.

It passed from leasehold to freehold around 1600 and was later added to the Wyndham Estates.

A 19th century house with formal landscaped gardens now stands on the site - see Walk No. 12, Felon's Oak, for details of Croydon Hall.

Just past the building a fingerpost points RH to Golsoncott, the lane leads past the old stables behind Croydon Hall. The path winds round to the left in front of a barn conversion and then continues down the lane to a stile. Here, the field is more like parkland, indeed it used to be part of Croydon Estate, and beautiful specimen trees are landscaped into the scenery.

The path crosses the field to the gateway below. Over the stile (no waymarks here) the next gate and stile appear in the right front as you walk forward in a straight line. Just before you reach it enjoy the sight of a circle of beech trees on the LH side. Cross into the next field and follow the LH hedge.

Through the trees you can catch glimpses of a lake and if you peep through the leaves swans and cygnets can sometimes be seen swimming gracefully over the water. The lake is in part of the private grounds of Golsoncott House hidden in trees on the LH.

At the hedge's far end there is yet another stile. Over it, there are no signs to help you. A track leads down the meadow but this is not the footpath. The field opposite has a small gate in its RH topmost corner appearing to lead into the ditch! Open (and close) this and walk along the ridge (the path obviously used to run along the ditch) on the RH of the field, it leads down to the road in Golsoncott, where there is a fingerpost and gate. The stream, fed from the spring above, runs down through the field and races through a bed of watercress. Turn LH up the lane, which has a miscellany of different ferns, mosses and liverworts on the shady banks, and 5 minutes' walk will bring Forche's Garden into view.

[Walked in February]

61

Walk No. 12

Graded : EASY but with some uphill.
Special Feature ~ the Luxborough Valley

ST 018 389   2 miles [3 km.] 1½ hrs
Felon's Oak to Tacker Street, Roadwater, returning to Croydon.
By road, from the A39 at Dragon Cross take the Roadwater
turning, after ¾ mile turn right, sign-posted Croydon Hall. Keep
straight on - the road ends at Felon's Oak after 2 miles.
There is room to park without obstructing field entrances.

It is possible that those using wheelchairs could
access the first part of this footpath. However,
this section just past Croydon Hall is possibly
too steep for the ones that require pushing. In
dry conditions those with motorised chairs and
families with pushchairs could reach the barn
where there are excellent views in all directions.

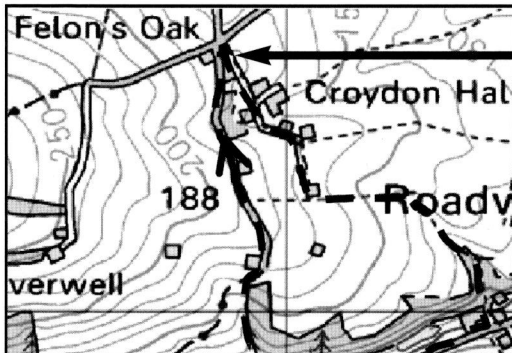

62

START: Walk through the stone pillars towards Croydon Hall. *The second large tree in the avenue (over the wall on the RH) is the rare Foxglove Tree, Paulownia tomentosa, look for its very large heart-shaped leaves.*

Croydon Hall appears on the LH as you continue down the road. *There was a settlement recorded in Croydon in 1221. After the foundation of Cleeve Abbey the monks received the estate of various holdings including Croydon. Through the centuries the property remained a farm, it was converted from leasehold to freehold in 1600 and later added to the Wyndham Estates. The farm was enlarged and turned into a gentleman's residence at the end of the 19th century, becoming Croydon Hall. Later it was sold to a German nobleman, Count Hochberg, who had to leave when the First World War broke out. During the last war the Hall became a school and housed evacuees. Later, still a school, run by Bristol Education Authority, it catered for 'children in need'. Now it is a '**Holistic Venue and Training Centre (01984) 640052**. An Osho oasis in Somerset'.*

Keep the Hall on your left and continue on past the pine trees to Home Cottage. Turn RH going along the field edge towards a barn, just before you reach it, go through the field gate (fingerpost on RH) and then turn left, walking down the hedge-line on a grassy path.

The Field Scabious, Knautia arvensis, and the pink Musk Mallow, Malva moschata, can be found among the more common hedgerow plants. The view towards the Brendon Hills extends to Timwood and Comberow on the right-hand horizon and straight ahead Kingsdown Clump caps the skyline. Nestling in the hills on the right Leighland comes into focus as you proceed further down the field.

Follow the hedge-line round the corner then pass through a gateway at the bottom still keeping to the field edge. As the wood comes nearer, a stile and hunting gate come into view. Once over them and into the wood good examples of some of our native trees can be seen growing here, beech, maple, sycamore, and holly. The stony path (a stream bed in winter) goes steeply downhill, the banks lined with the Male Fern, Dryopteris filix-mas, and Hart's Tongue, Asplenium scolopendrium.

Walk down through the shady wood (ignore side turnings to the LH and RH) and at the bottom pass beside Croydon Cottage (on the right) then bear left over a wooden bridge and pass a cottage (on the left). This is Tacker Street, the name coming from Vale Mill just down the valley, which used to be a Tucking Mill. The lane leads to the road.

Immediatedly on the RH is the entrance to **Roadwater Fishery**. On the LH side is **Bill Poirrier's Blacksmith's Craft Workshop (01984 640648)** where items of traditional ironwork are made on the premises. Visitors are welcome to the Craft Workshop. Opposite the blacksmith is Glasses Farm.

Turn right and walk along the road towards Luxborough.

This is the beginning of the Luxborough Valley. This deeply wooded combe is wonderful at any time of the year but in the autumn, spectacular. The soil's acidic properties are indicated by the presence of Whortleberry, Vaccinium myrtillus in the hedge and specimens of the Hard Fern, Blechnum spicant, beginning to appear further on. As you walk watch out for herons visiting the well stocked fish ponds of Roadwater Fishery below.

Ten minutes along the road, edged by a splendid beech hedge and with the sight and sound of the Washford River below, brings you to Peterswell Lake Cottage.

A fingerpost on the LH points to Treborough Lane and Fellon's Oak (strange spelling!) Cross the road and follow the footpath down the LH side of the house and keep on bearing leftwards. Follow the Washford River for a little along a muddy path.

Turn RH crossing the river over a wide bridge made of poles and planks.

On both sides there is an expanding area of Japanese Knotweed, Fallopia japonica; this is an alien weed impossible to check.

Bear left after crossing the bridge and continue upwards under the canopy of the massive trees.

There is a large horse chestnut tree beside the path and the tall leaning larch trees on the left look like they have ivy skirts draped around them. An ancient oak grows near a beautiful beech, which in the summer has woodland butterflies flitting around it.

The track continues round to the right but the footpath goes straight ahead and upwards through a gate on the LH side.

The brambles and nettles can become a little overgrown as the path ascends through a steep meadow; it originally ran along the edge of the wood but dense growth now forces you to walk further out.

In the hedge are several stands of Dogwood, Cornus sanguinea. The lush meadow itself is a wildlife haven – in spring it is covered with Lady's-smock, Cardamine pratense, and in autumn vivid flashes of purple Hardheads, Centaurea nigra, dot the field.

Legs ache as you climb the meadow but the view behind over Treborough woods is a good reason to pause and breathe in the fresh air from the Brendon Hills. The site of the Treborough slate quarry in the woodland opposite is now completely masked by trees.

The gate out of the field is visible at the far end and on its right is a small apple orchard that is part of a nearby cottage garden.

Climb the stile into the sunken trackway, called Greenland Lane, and turn right until you come to Greenland Cottage then turn sharp left onto the lane's tarmac surface.

Walking up the lane, at the point where it levels out, you can see on both sides there are thin strips of ground lying between two hedges. These strips of land were once cultivated by farm workers, who having laboured all day in the fields, came home and slaved in their own gardens to grow produce for themselves. These strips were in cultivation about 60 years ago but are now returning to nature.

There are two ways back to Felon's Oak

A little further on a fingerpost on the right points over the field to the barn.

Opposite the stile grows a patch of Hops, Humulus lupulus; if they are in flower it is worth stopping to smell the sweet scent. In the ditch under the hops there used to be a pond full of tadpoles and newts but this is now sadly drained through road improvements.

Climb over the stile and cross the field to the barn.

Turning LH at the barn brings you back to Croydon Hall.

Or, keep straight on along Greenland Lane for an alternative way back. After about ¼ mile, just before you reach a wall bounding Croydon Gardens, a sharp turn to the RH (fingerpost points the way) leads down a path alongside some greenhouses. The path joins the roadway from Croydon Hall passing through a stone arch. Turn LH and within a few minutes you are back at Felon's Oak.

[Walked in May]

The possibility of the Felon's Oak being a hanging tree is of course the subject of much speculation but facts as to its real place in history are hard to find. There are other hanging trees in the area, notably the Heddon Oak, sadly now gone. Located between Crowcombe and Stogumber, it possibly had a connection with the grisly workings of Judge Jeffreys after the Monmouth Rebellion.
The Felon's Oak is said to have had a sheep-stealer hung from its boughs and its place and prominence (at a crossroads) may give some credence to this.
A map detailing the Ancient Hundreds of Carhampton, by J. Savage, shows the oak as a boundary mark and here named as Fellows Oak. The original Felon's Oak has gone but has been replaced with a new tree - a traditional landmark for the 21st century.

Male Fern	*Hard Fern*	*Hart's-tongue Fern*
Dryopteris	*Blechnum*	*Asplenium*
filix-mas	*spicant*	*scolopendrium*

Walk No. 13

Graded : CHALLENGING (with considerable amount of uphill)
Special feature ~ Panoramic view at highpoint of 952 ft.

ST 032 383   4½ miles [7½ km]   2¼ hours
Roadwater to Chidgley over Kingsdown Clump, and return.
🚌 The walk starts in the centre of Roadwater at the village hall
(on the LH side coming from Washford). It is possible to park
alongside the recreation ground where the road is wider.
*The walk passes through most beautiful countryside, and intertwines
with three of the footpaths of Nettlecombe parish. Its heights show
West Somerset's hills, valleys, wooded combes and seascape to full
advantage and at certain points near Kingsdown Clump the view is
unrivalled in distance and diversity.*

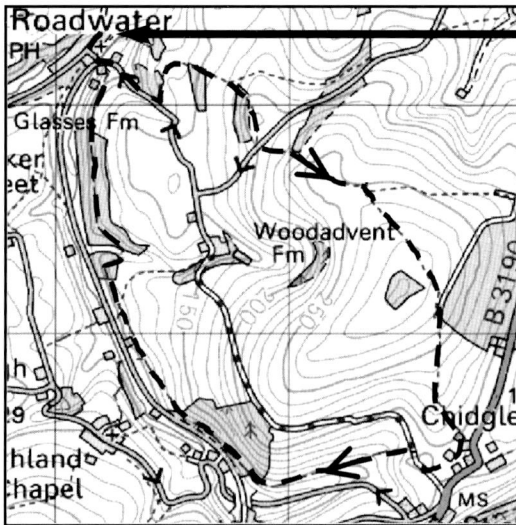

START: Walk along the road past the post office.
*On the LH can be found the Methodist Chapel. The original
'Ebenezer' chapel dating from 1842 was replaced in 1907 by the
present building, now serving a small and faithful congregation.*

Turn LH into Station Lane ('Road Ahead Narrows to 9 ft') and walk between the houses for about 100 yards until you can see the track of the Mineral Line on either side.

If you look over the gate to the left you can see the bridge support girders over the Washford River which formed the old railway crossing, and 100 yards behind it the brick-built single-story dwelling, now converted to a bungalow, which was Roadwater's Mineral Line station.

Follow the lane, called Harper's Lane, up the hill - on the right is a fingerpost, the RH arm pointing to Chidgley Valley - the return will bring us back here.

In spring, the raised bank on the RH is carpeted with Wood Anemone, Anemone nemorosa and Wood-sorrel, Oxalis acetosella.

Ten minutes uphill leads us to a stile on the LH with a fingerpost sign pointing to Chidgley via Kingsdown. The track goes up through the middle of the wood and yellow waymarks appear on the oak trees lining the path.

At the end of the wood, there is a gateway and stile on the RH, but first, take a few minutes to peep through the trees at the edge of the LH field to look back and see an unusual view of Roadwater village.

Return to the stile and go into the RH field, keep to the LH hedge for 25 yards or so and a new gateway and stile appear immediately in front of you. Over this one, head for the horizon up the RH hedge and past some fine veteran oaks on the way. This is where the walk begins its test of stamina; for the next mile the walk continues up a series of connecting fields, ever steeper. The necessary rests can be attributed to interest in the unfolding panorama behind.

There is a stile in the top RH corner of the field – this is pheasant country and unexpected meetings cause mutual surprise!

Still keep to the RH edge of the field and a small hunting gate leads into the next field – there are, as yet, no waymark signs here but keep going up to the crest of the hill.

The top of this field yields a panoramic view, with the Welsh coastline, Brean Down and the Mendip hills over to the right; the Quantock Hills, Watchet, Washford and Cleeve Abbey in the foreground;

Minehead, presently disfigured by its white wart, to the left; in the middle, Rodhuish Common and away to the far left lie the wooded Brendon Hills.

Once at the top you can see a farm track going upwards over the fields in the middle distance. However, still keeping to the RH hedge the footpath has been diverted down to a stile and dog gate in the far corner leading into Wood Advent Lane. Turn LH and 50 yards further on a fingerpost points to the RH into the farm track. Follow the track upwards through an opening and fork immediately right into yet another field.

Here the path follows the line of the LH hedge - made up of a mixture of native beech and holly. There are a number of 'creep holes' in the hedge fashioned by animals, and their little paths contour horizontally along the field.

Cresting the rise look straight ahead and Kingsdown Clump comes into view.

Keep to the LH (walking towards the Quantocks) until a stile in the next hedge becomes visible. The fingerpost indicates Roadwater behind, Nettlecombe LH and Chidgley RH.

Turn RH and go into the next field over a stile.

This is farming country and animals are permanently grazing so especial care is needed when passing amongst them and in closing gates (or indeed, leaving them open if they are found open).

The path now takes a diagonal course to a metal gate and wooden stile complex with an ancient fingerpost leaning alongside.

Kingsdown Clump (spot-height 952 feet) projects at the top of the field to the RH while the path goes straight across the middle of the field to the LH of the trees.

It has to be said, the beech, sycamore, ash and scots pine, which comprise the Kingsdown Clump, are more imposing from a distance than from close quarters! However, those who might visit in spring-time would be amazed at the carpet of bluebells which cover the drab undergrowth.

The view backwards recedes as a new one comes into focus with the Sticklepath and Chidgley around the corner.

Below on the LH lies Kings Wood and here a difficulty emerges. The original footpath passed straight to the wood below beside a hedge that has been since removed. However, make for the RH end of Kings Wood where it meets a hedge that is still in existence and turn right along the track in front of the hedge and walk to the corner where a wide farm track leads downwards.

Ahead and below **Chidgley Manor Farm (01984 640378)** *offering traditional farmhouse bed and breakfast accommodation, can be seen on the other side of the road.*

The footpath used to go straight to the road to the left of the thatched cottage directly below and most maps still show this as the route. However, an official diversion has been made and a new path opened, so keep to the farm track, which now leads to the right, until you come to the gate just before the farmyard and outbuildings of Chidgley Hill Farm.

Pass over the stile next to the metal gate and 25 paces ahead go through another metal gate. The fingerpost denotes Roadwater via Kingsdown 2 ¼ and Roadwater Valley route. This is the halfway point and it is mostly downhill ahead!

Turn sharply right, through another metal gate following the Roadwater Valley route.

Continue along the green track until you come to the junction with another track. This green lane is a byway open to vehicles from Chidgley to Wood Advent.

Cross the lane and a gate opposite, marked with a blue waymark, leads into a grassy field. Keep a big oak tree on the LH and keeping in the same field cross to the RH hedge where the bridleway continues through the field beside the leafy canopy.

Red Admiral butterflies flutter about and add to the beauty of the peaceful scene. Comberow and The Incline appear on the LH with Hook Hill perching on the hillside in front. There are numerous opportunities for a picnic stop all along this section and I have named this part 'Willow Walk' because there are a number of large willow trees between here and Roadwater. There is Salix caprea, Goat Willow, Salix cinerea, Rusty Sallow, and all hybrids in between – in early spring their catkins drop pollen from overhead.

Entry to Pit Wood is by a gate. Nettlecombe's paths and Old Cleeve's intertwine for the next mile passing from one parish to the other at least four times. Go on downwards (ignoring a RH fork) through the mixed conifers and broad-leaved trees. Tracks bisect at a clearing and a fingerpost informs that this is a bridleway. Keep straight on for a short distance and another post points onwards to Roadwater. To the immediate left a steep path leads downwards to Pitt Mill and on to Leighland. However, do not deviate, keep straight on through the wood leaving it by a wooden gate at the end.

Beyond Pit Wood the path, lined with willows and dog roses, opens out and wends its way along the top of the steeply sloping fields. The Mineral Line, running parallel with the footpath, is visible below and the river very audible. Leighland Church is perched above at head height across the valley.

The path takes a lower level over the field (past a lone waymarked post) and enters Nap Wood. The beech and oaks give way to coniferous darkness and then the path emerges into a small boggy field with a stream to cross and returns to the wood – now Erridge Wood, gloomy, with dark spruce trees - but back in Old Cleeve Parish. Keep straight on, joining a main track on the left.

Exit the wood by a small gate onto a grassy track along a sloping field with Roadwater in view ahead.

The gate at the far end leads back into Harper's Lane, which was noted at the start, then LH to Station Road and RH to the Recreation Ground.

[Walked in May]

Goat Willow – Salix caprea   *Rusty Sallow – Salix cinerea*

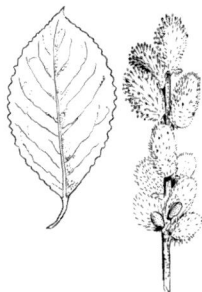

Walk No. 14

Graded : EASY (with some uphill)
Special feature ~ Fern-lined, mossy sunken lane

ST 030 382   1½ miles [2½ km]   1¼ hours
Roadwater to Higher Hayne and returning via Stamborough.
🚌 Park in the Valiant Soldier car park behind the inn - you can
then visit the pub for refreshment before or after your walk.

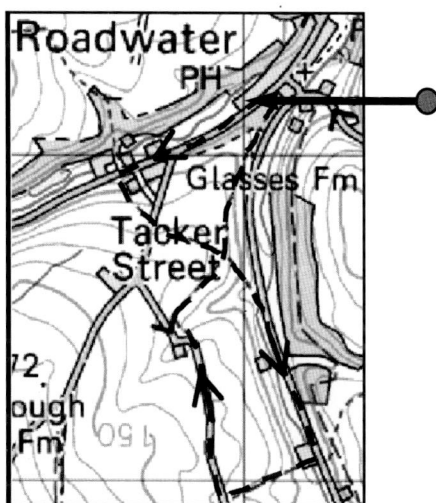

The Valiant Soldier (01984 640223) *provides good food from 12
noon to 2 p.m. and between 6 p.m. and 9 p.m. (7 – 9 on Sundays)
and welcomes walkers for refreshment. This inn is a valuable part of
Roadwater's history and has served the community for centuries.
The inn sign is the work of the late Rachel Reckitt (see walk No.11).*
START: Walk to the far end of Roadwater. A little further up the
road divides, LH to Treborough and RH to Luxborough. Walk
along the RH road to **Glasses Farm.** *This is a traditional
farmhouse, part of which dates from the 16th century. The farm now
provides livery for local people and this walk passes through many of its
fields.* Immediately past the farm entrance a fingerpost on the LH

points the way up a flight of wooden steps. The stile at the top of the steps leads into a little sloping meadow – no signs but common sense leads walkers over the field to the gate in the opposite hedge.

Pass through this gate (with a fingerpost on left) and then on through another gate on the RH and into another meadow. Cross this field on the left side to a stile in the opposite corner with a good view of Roadwater nestling in its wooded valley. The stile here leads down to the road via a short steep cleft, turn RH for 50 yards and then LH into a field (this gate may have to be climbed) with a fingerpost pointing out the direction of the footpath. The path leads straight over the field. Take for your direction the circle of trees on the far skyline (Kingsdown Clump).

In front is Erridge Wood, a dark mass of conifers, with Leighland Church and settlement in the RH distance.

Ahead is a gate and stile leading to a sloping buttercup meadow with the Mineral Line below.

A graceful oak contrasts with the serried ranks of conifers and primroses and a sprinkling of bluebells in spring give way to lady's-smock and summer meadow flowers in this unspoilt pasture.

Another gate and stile lead onto the Mineral Line. Here turn RH and pass the Traphole Water Treatment Works in its alcove of larches. *On the LH large clumps of yellow broom scent the air and little paths lead into the wood's secret places – perfect for children.* Scan the interesting names of the houses as you pass, Traphole, Crystal Glen, Glen Haven and then, after about ten minutes walking, Lower Hayne. Here a fingerpost points the way RH through a garden gate and then into a garden and finally through a kissing gate. Cross the river bridge and follow the winding path up the hill into the sunken lane.

Outcrops of shale appear in the LH bank. The steep sides are lined with mosses and liverworts with pale green ferns lightening the gully. Dry stone walls interweave with the natural shale and here and there on the LH modern drainage outlets have been carefully fashioned to fit in with the original walling, an ancient and modern partnership that really works. In May, the whole lane is lined with Ramsons, Allium ursinum, their garlic-perfumed flowers reflect the filtered sunlight as you walk up through a fragrant sea of white - the subject of the cover photograph.

At the top of the lane, turn RH into the road, called Ham Lane, and walk until a sharp bend is reached.

Here, above the field on warm summer days, larks trill out their happiness – in this quiet unspoilt area there are perfect habitats for much of our beleagured wildlife and it is good to know that the land is cared for in a way which allows flora and fauna to thrive.

One of the fields here had a 'crop' of Field Pansy, Viola arvensis, a rare sight anywhere. The roadside banks are home for more wild flowers than you can count, plus bees, butterflies, beetles and mice; best of all, little traffic pollutes the air.

A field gate on the RH just before Ham Lane Reservoir has a fingerpost pointing over the field. The gate opens and ahead in the field you can see a grassy path through the middle. Do not use this! Keep to the LH and clamber up the steep slope of the field to the top hedge and here the footpath runs all along the hedge, its height affording the best view of all. Eventually, on the LH you come to a gate that you came through earlier. Pass it by and keep it on the LH. The footpath continues over a stile with a good-sized Rowan tree, Sorbus aucuparia, on the RH. As you descend through the wood you join another footpath, this one coming from Roadwater and going to Leighland via the Mineral Line. Keep going leftwards - looking across the valley you can see the now-restored Temperance Hall.

The Temperance Hall was built in 1877 by Sir Walter Trevelyan, who was President of the United Temperance Alliance, on the site of the old blade mill. It was used for meetings, entertainments and then became a clubroom for men and boys. It is now a private residence.

The wood is called Road Wood; the track can be boggy after rain and leads steeply downhill to Roadwater. The fingerpost on the roadside says 'Public Footpath to Leighland Chapel'- turn LH back to The Valiant Soldier and enjoy a cooling (or warming) drink.

[Walked in May]

Walk No. 15

Graded : EASY (with some uphill)
Special features ~ Landscape and magnificent trees

ST 057 377   2 miles [3¼ km.]   1½ hours
Nettlecombe Court to Chidgley Farm. By road to Nettlecombe
Lodge then returning to Nettlecombe Court.
🚌 From Tropiquaria at Washford Cross, take the B 3190
signposted Bampton. At the first crossroads, Fair Cross, turn LH
until you reach Woodford. Turn RH and then after 200 yards
follow sign into The Leonard Wills Field Centre, Nettlecombe
Court.
This walk is within the boundaries of Exmoor National Park -
partly in Old Cleeve parish and partly in Nettlecombe.
Park under trees below the church.

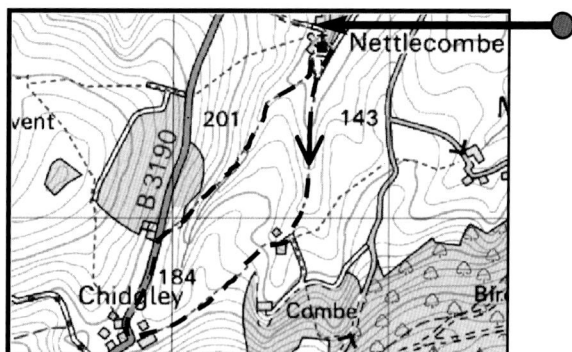

*You may wish to go inside Nettlecombe church, which is truly an
English gem. Amongst other treasures, it has notable stone effigies.
One, dating from 1260, is of Sir Simon Ralegh who has his legs
crossed indicating that he went on the Crusades. Next to it is the tomb
of Sir John Ralegh, who died in 1387, together with his lady.
Sir John, exceptionally tall, was known as the seven-foot giant.*

The east window was installed in memory of Sir Walter John Trevelyan, 1866-1931. It represents the four seasons and also shows the Trevelyan horse.

In the churchyard, under the north wall a rare plant grows. It is called Kraus's Clubmoss, Selaginella kraussiana, and looks like a tiny green fern. (Time given for the walk does not include a stop here.)

START: Go through the two columns, one horse's head is missing- perhaps being restored.

The Trevelyan horses are commemorated at Nettlecombe because an early Trevelyan was supposed to have been saved from drowning by a quick-thinking horse which supported his master in the water.

On the RH lies Nettlecombe Court. It is let to the Leonard Wills Field Studies Council as a centre for the study of natural history.

Nettlecombe was recorded in the Domesday Book in 1086 as belonging to Earl Godwin before the Norman Conquest. After its forfeiture to the Crown the land was conveyed to Hugh de Ralegh between 1154 and 1165. Since that time Nettlecombe has never been sold, passing by descent through the families of Ralegh, Whalesborough, Trevelyan and Wolseley.

The house is a Tudor manor house erected in 1599 on the site of a previous house. It has a late-medieval kitchen, fine hall and minstrel's gallery and, although not open to the public, can be viewed by appointment.

Begin the walk by keeping straight ahead up the drive with the house away on the RH.

Note the field above on the LH, apart from the splendid specimens of unusual trees it has some rather special thistles growing there. Two common species, the Creeping Thistle and the Marsh Thistle, have combined to form a rare hybrid, Cirsium x celakovskianum – there is only one other record of this one in Somerset.

Climb over the metal rails of the stile ahead; the gate is marked 'No horses, bikes or vehicles'.

Follow the track, which can be boggy, passing more fine examples of trees, including a copper beech on the LH and a Wild Cherry ahead. The landscaped park delights the eye in every direction.

On the RH a wired compound intrigues, and investigation rewards the inquisitive. A stone edifice surmounts a trough and water supply. The Latin inscription translates as follows:

> *"But the water which I shall give you, yea it shall become in him*
> *a fountain (or spring) of water flowing into eternal life".*

The inscription also bears the following words:

> *"Erected by John Trevelyan of Yarnscombe who married Avice*
> *the heiress of Champernowne and Valletort and of Edmund,*
> *Earl of Cornwall and died 1558."*

A pond on the opposite side is known as Parsonage Pond and is used for field studies by the Centre.

Walking onwards, pass through a metal gate system and over a stile to the RH of a wooden gate. Straight ahead on the skyline is Pooke Wood, and on the left, the valley where Combe Cottage hides away. Climbing gradually uphill the 'parting of the ways' is reached marked by a fingerpost to Chidgley, Monksilver and Nettlecombe.

Turn RH down the road keeping the house on your LH. Pass immediately RH under an arched cherry tree and the next fingerpost appears. A little uphill another stile awaits climbing and on the LH a magnificent oak tree guards the track. The path follows the RH fence line (small diversions may be required through this wooded section as fallen boughs sometimes block the path). However, the top of the field presents a pastoral view over the wooded landscape of Nettlecombe Parish as you join Old Cleeve Parish. Cross over an unusual double stile into the field and enjoy the extensive view to the north over the Severn Estuary. Here the direction is not at all obvious but keep upwards to the middle horizon. A field gate with no waymarks or signs leads onto the track to Chidgley Farm, which is soon reached. Pass through the farmyard, being sensitively aware of the needs of the working community and animals here, and out to the road. Turn RH and <u>with care</u> follow the <u>very</u> busy road back to the house on the LH, which is Nettlecombe Lodge (a ten minute road walk). Opposite the Lodge, go through a field gate (fingerpost points to Nettlecombe). Turn left going down the grassy track into the trees and over the stile at the yellow waymark. Some of these oaks are veteran trees and are numbered as such. A track appears ahead and yellow waymarks are painted on growing trees. Cross the track and go down the grassy path past the fingerpost pointing back the way you have come. Ignore the stiles which punctuate the RH hedge line – they provide private access to the land below.

*Opportunities for picnics abound, and there are many places for children to play safely in a natural environment. However, a **word of warning** to parents of little children who love running ahead - be aware of the stream below.*

Woodpeckers drum from massive trees if you come in summertime. After passing through the first gate, one architectural monster, a fallen oak, lies on the RH providing a fine habitat for beetles, ants, grubs and fungi and an outdoor laboratory for students.

Almost at the bottom the stream has been diverted to accommodate a flow meter, monitoring and recording water levels for the Field Centre's scientists. During April a native wild cherry or Gean, Prunus avium, sprinkles petal confetti from above and signs of it still remain on the grass underneath.

In every direction wonderful specimens of mature trees tower above. Some of these are very rare and very old and must have been planted centuries ago. In the grounds of Nettlecombe Court, it is said that a line of English oaks was planted to replace those cut down to supply timber for our navy at the time of the Spanish Armada in 1588. These replacement oaks must therefore be some of the oldest in England.

Pass through a second gate and so into the meadows that surround the Field Centre, keeping to the stream bank continue to the fence at the end.

Notice the slate flagstones covering the stream; no doubt they were obtained from Treborough slate quarries, which were once owned by the Trevelyan family.

Go over the stile and return to the car parked beside the church.

[Walked in May]

Walk No.16

Graded : MODERATE
Special feature ～ Tranquility

ST 033 371   3 miles [4¾ km]   2 hours
Mineral Line to Wood Advent, Chidgley, Kingsdown Clump,
returning to Wood Advent and Mineral Line at Higher Hayne.
🚌 In Roadwater, travelling from Washford, 100 yards after the
shop, turn LH into Station Road (no road name but sign says
'Road ahead narrows to 9 feet'). Oatway Cottage on the RH was
built in 1700. Turn RH along the Mineral Line. (Sign : No
Through Road.) After ¾ mile stop at Lower Hayne and park
opposite Hillview Cottage - beyond the oak tree there is room for
cars. Please park sensitively – if the needs of the residents are
respected they will, of course, welcome you to their area.
(Alternatively, and better still, park in Roadwater and walk up the
Mineral Line to the start point.)

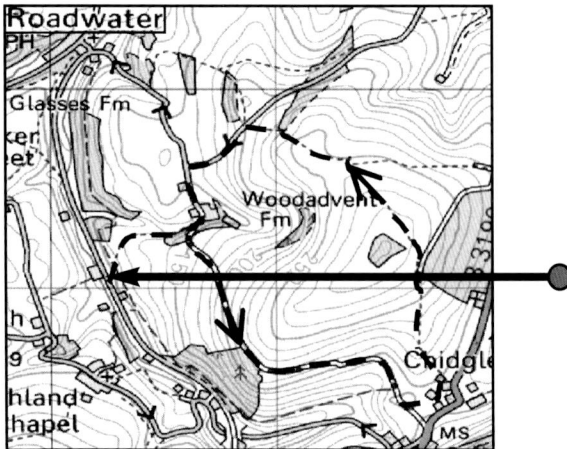

START: Under the oak tree a fingerpost points up the hill. Once
over the stile if you take 30 paces to the RH you can see the path
leading to the LH and upwards towards a lone oak near the top

of the field with a post just below it. At the very top, pass a gate on the RH and keeping the dry-stone wall and hedge also on your RH, continue round until you are on the track which leads into the wood ahead. The river – a tributary feeding the Washford River - can be seen and heard in a channel through the field below.

Enter the wooded lane over a stile and walk up the lane, lined with native holly trees and grounded on the shale bedrock, until you arrive at a junction with another track. LH goes to Wood Advent Farm and the RH goes uphill to Chidgley via Pit Wood. Turn RH into the lane leading up the hill.

This lane is a byway open to vehicles – and it is possible that you may meet tractors, motorbikes, mountain bikes or even 4-wheel drive cars. In practice it is unlikely that you will meet any vehicle on the entire walk – the special feature of the walk is listed as 'tranquillity'. (By some mischance if you choose the day a motorbike rally is passing this way – peace may temporarily be missing.)

Walking up the green lane, pausing for breath, a backward look shows the sea gleaming in the far distance.

The banks are lined with wild flowers in most seasons - in late summer pink Herb Robert, Geranium robertianum, sprawls over the banks and underfoot Red Bartsia, Odontitis vernus, pokes through the red soil – this is an interesting annual plant partly parasitic on the roots of grasses. On the RH a bird's-eye view of Leighland appears and makes a good photograph.

The top end of Pit Wood is reached and is entered via a gate (this is roughly the half-way point to Chidgley) and in a little while a second gate leads out of the wood.

There is quite a variety of fungi growing on the dead and decaying wood. Lower down the slopes, in September, a Brain Fungus, Sparassis crispa was found. This fungus is also called Cauliflower Fungus and is rather rare – it is found growing at the base of conifers. It can be eaten after careful cleaning and is such a delicacy that anyone who has tried it once will be hooked for life.

Do not be tempted into eating any fungi unless you are sure they are identified correctly. Checking in a book with a photograph is not sufficient – the Death Cap looks quite like a mushroom. Ask an expert and if you can't find one, don't risk it - it is better to be safe than sorry.

Once out of the wood there is another gate leading into the continuation of the lane and here it becomes grassy underfoot. Continue for about ½ mile, the eventual end of the lane is where it joins the road on the Sticklepath. However, turn LH before that point when you come to a diversion, which is clearly marked as a permissive path. The grassy path over the field ahead avoids the busy road and leads straight to Chidgley Hill Farm.

After going through one metal gate turn back LH through another gate with the fingerpost pointing to Roadwater via Kingsdown.

After a further 25 yards a stile over the track is the last obstruction. The way ahead is uphill and friendly cows may come and investigate you and even lick your hand for a salty snack.

Continue on the track moving towards Kingsdown Clump entering the next field through a gate where the footpath crosses the field to the corner of King's Wood. However, the track provides a sensible route for a little further until you come to a hedge end on the RH, then turn RH along the hedge until you reach the corner of King's Wood. Here make your way between the wood and the clump, proceeding upwards across the field. As you reach the top of the rise you can see a gate at the junction of the RH and LH hedges (with Dunster Beach framed in the background).

Over the stile the view is stunning – a perfect picnic place. Buzzards quarter the skies overhead. The sun shining through their feathers make their wings appear almost transparent.

Cross the field (aiming for far-distant Minehead) to another stile (a little one) and then 50 yards later a stile on the LH leads into another field. Near the stile there is a fingerpost indicating footpaths to Nettlecombe, Chidgley and Roadwater.

Once over the stile make your way towards Roadwater round the field beside the RH hedge, ignoring sundry gaps to the RH and finally, once over the horizon, pass down a slope with an extended view up the Luxborough Valley on the LH.

Leave the field on a stony track, which continues downhill through another field, until a gate is reached giving access onto Wood Advent Lane.

At this point turn LH and walk down the lane until its junction with Harper's Lane.

In the hedgerow a very pretty wildflower is found in late summer. The pink petals of the Musk Mallow, Malva moschata, are very eye-catching and rather more unusual and beautiful than its widespread relation the Common Mallow, Malva sylvestris.

Turn LH down the lane into the farmyard.

Wood Advent Farm (01984 640920) *was built in 1804 and enjoys a peaceful location away from the beaten track.*

Mr. & Mrs. J. Brewer offer traditional Bed and Breakfast accommodation in this delightful and secluded location. Wood Advent, being both within the boundaries of Exmoor National Park and nestling into the Brendon Hills, is ideally suited for those who love walking and appreciate the natural beauty of this area.

The lane passes right through the yard of the working farm, so caution should be exercised - dogs must of course remain on leads. Keep the farmhouse on the RH, passing a pond on the LH and walk up the hill. In a little while you will arrive back at the starting point of the green lane and the fingerpost.

Turn RH down the track, over the stile, into the field, retracing your steps and contouring back down the grassy slope to Lower Hayne.

[Walked in September]

Cauliflower Fungus
Sparassis
crispa

PITT MILL

Walk No. 17

Graded : EASY (short, but with two steep wooded climbs)
Special feature ~ Working Water Mill

ST 034 369   1 mile [1¾ km]   1 hour
Mineral Line to Leighland Chapel, Maggoty Lane to Pitt Mill,
through Pit Woods to Lower Hayne. (Note spelling, one 't' for the
wood and two for the mill!)

🚐 In Roadwater (travelling from Washford) pass the Village Hall,
Post Office and telephone box and turn first LH into Station Road.
50 yds in turn RH along the Mineral Line. After ¾ mile stop at
Higher Hayne. Parking along the edge of the Mineral Line is
possible where there are wider parts but please avoid using up
parking areas set aside for vehicles belonging to residents.
Alternatively, park in Roadwater and walk to the start point.

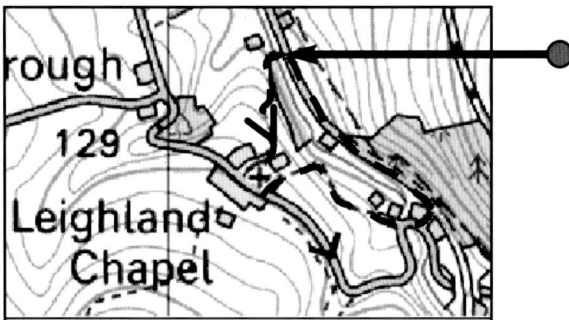

START: The footpath begins on the RH side (the fingerpost is
hidden behind a cherry tree 'Bridleway to Leighland'). The
footpath is named 'The Rocks'- the reason quickly becoming
obvious.
Cross the river bridge and follow the lane as it meanders round to
the left. The shale bedrock is visible along the path as you pass
steeply upwards through an ancient coppiced wood. The eroded
gully is very slippery and boggy underfoot, even in good conditions.

Ferns, mosses, liverworts and lichens carpet the banks and naturally harmonise with shade loving plants such as navelwort.

After about 10 minutes a small, disused quarry is passed on the RH then the path turns around to the LH, soon reaching the small settlement of Leighland. A RH turn takes you into the lane - keep straight on until you reach the road. Note the garden walls made of shale, possibly quarried from the little quarry below. Turning to the LH, 'Leighland Chapel' is ahead on the LH. The latter is St. Giles' Church, built in 1865 to accommodate the large mining population and now lovingly cared for by a very small faithful community.

The original Chapel of St. Giles of Leigh was of ancient foundation, probably dating from Saxon times and was served by the monks of Cleeve Abbey. For more details see the 'Two Churches Walk' or better still, go inside and read the excellent leaflet entitled "St.Giles', Leighland, A Short History". The church is open in daytime and a peaceful but interesting pause can be spent inside.

To continue the walk, from the church porch (note the swallows' nests in the rafters) turn LH onto the footpath which passes down through the churchyard, through a small gate and into Maggoty Lane. Continue to the RH and downhill, (slippery when wet) past a house on the LH, until a stile is reached. The shady lane opens up into a sloping field, in spring full of wildflowers with the sound of the Washford River adding another dimension.

The path follows the hedge line towards the farm ahead. Here the footpath has been diverted away from the farmyard and now goes through a gate into the orchard, crosses in a straight line between the trees, and leaves it by a gate to the farm track below (fingerpost). Bear RH and walk past the open barn into Pit Lane and then turn immediately LH.

In the lane there is a celebration of wild flowers – bluebells, foxgloves, pink campion and blue carpets of speedwell. In the autumn a number of different ferns drape the banks; a particularly fine one is the Lady Fern, Athyrium filix-femina.

At the bottom, on the right, the leat serving Pitt Mill tinkles past and, if you are lucky, dragonflies dart around the waterscape.

Turn sharp LH going past a Nissen hut attached to a barn until you arrive at Pitt Mill. Here a thriving business is based.

Two Rivers (01984 641028) *makes handmade paper using the water wheel for part of the process - it is an impressive sight to see the water mill working. Please ask if you wish to have a close look.*

This is not a craft shop but a cottage industry although you will be made welcome, especially if you purchase some of their unique, high-quality paper. Two Rivers opens from 9 a.m. to 4.30 p.m. and at weekends. Extra time is needed here to see all there is to see.

Eventually, make your way up the slope to the Mineral Line where the footpath (fingerpost - Footpath to Chidgley) goes straight opposite and up the bank into the wood where yellow waymarks painted on trees point the way. 100 yards of very steep climbing through deep leaf litter, going leftwards at first, brings you out to a wide track and here another fingerpost points out the route of the bridleway : RH to Chidgley and the LH to Roadwater.

Turn LH and follow the path through the wood to a gate and then into the field. The boundary with Nettlecombe parish adjoins the path, which is girded by a drystone wall. Ancient beech trees sit atop the wall and form a leafy tunnel.

The Mineral Line can be seen below on the LH as you walk along close to the hedge-line.

Majestic buzzards patrol the grassy slopes for unsuspecting small mammals and as they soar up above Leighland on the other side of the valley you can see the colours and beautiful patterns of their under-feathers.

After about ¼ mile the first house that comes into view over the valley is Higher Hayne.

Just before you reach the point directly opposite the house, a grassy track cuts diagonally downwards through the field. This path is opposite a gap in the top RH hedge that you have been following and is easily missed if you are not looking for it.

At the bottom of the field a gate leads back into the Mineral Line and the end of a short but very peaceful walk.

[Walked in May]

Walk No. 18

Graded : EASY
Special feature ~ former grange of Cleeve Abbey

ST 033 366   2¾ miles   [5 km]   1½ hours
Leighland to Leigh Barton via Broadfield Wood and return.
🚌 At the first junction after the Valiant Soldier Inn at Roadwater,
take the LH turning signposted Treborough and Brendon Hill.
¼ mile up the hill take the first turning left to Leighland, which
is reached after 1 mile. 100 yards past St. Giles' church, a new
church car park, marked 'Private', has been made on the LH
(opposite Leighland Barn). Your car may be left here by kind
permission of Leighland Parochial Church Council (unless there
is a church function in progress in which case the car park may
be full.)

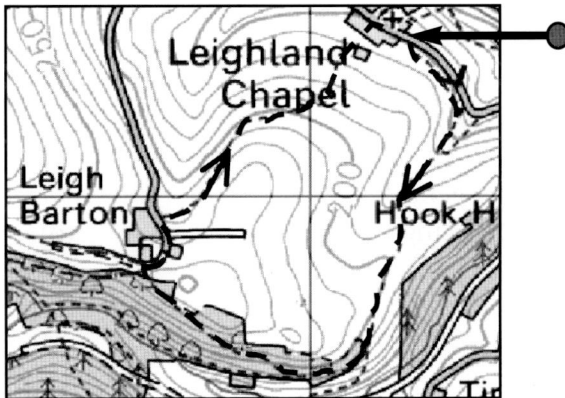

START : The footpath begins opposite the church car park at the
LH of the entrance to the house known as Leighland Barn.
Climb the stile and follow the lower hedge to the next stile. Or, if
you prefer, walk down the little lane to the bottom where you
can go over the first stile on the right into the field. Either way,
having arrived in the same field, cross the field upwards to the
large oak trees in the top LH corner.

86

The grass has some common wild flowers in the sward but also the Cut-leaved Crane's-bill, Geranium dissectum, which thrives on fertile soils and can be distinguished from other geraniums by the leaves as they are divided nearly to the base.

At the top hedge a stile sits under an oak tree and then 30 yards on the LH a gate and stile lead into a field. In this field, keep to the RH hedge and follow the field round, passing one gateway on a corner on the RH before coming to another gate. Go through this gate and keep to the RH hedge as you journey upwards.

On your LH you can see a covered reservoir – a flower-topped hump with a pink crest of Great Willowherb, known as 'Codlins and Cream', Epilobium hirsutum. There is a gate at the end of the field but no fingerpost or waymarks.

In August, a herd of Roe Deer was enjoying the barley planted in these fields. If you keep reasonably quiet, you too may be lucky enough to have a close encounter. They can be recognised by their white rumps as they bound away once they have seen you.

Standing with your back to the gate go straight across the field to the corner of the wood where there is another gate, this one leading into Broadfield Wood. The first section is scrubby but once properly in the wood the path diverges. The LH arm goes down the wood to Comberow, but take the RH to Leigh Barton. The path slopes gently downwards for a time passing through arches of holly lining the path. After about ¼ mile the track is joined by a path coming up on the LH from Comberow – yellow waymarks clearly visible.

The trees include beech, holly, sweet chestnut, larch and a mixture of conifers. Below, a wood warbler moves around in the high foliage. It is brightly coloured with moss green upperparts, pale yellow face/breast and strikingly pure white underparts. Earlier in the summer it would have sung its distinctive silvery song. Broadfield Wood, under the scrub, is known to be terraced. It is thought possible that in medieval times this area would have been used by the monastery for the cultivation of vines. It is a fact that the sheltered area here is almost totally frost-free, ideal for grapes that might have been nurtured in Comberow's medieval sun.

Keep straight on for about 50 yards to another junction and take the upward and RH fork. This becomes steep and then levels out into a wider track, finally exiting through a gate into Leigh Barton farm. Turn RH down through the farm buildings, down the lane, through a gate, keeping straight on downhill passing the house on the LH side.

Leigh Barton, known earlier as Leigh Grange, was one of the five granges of Cleeve Abbey. It is of late medieval origin and was enlarged in 1627 and further rebuilt in the classical style in 1811.

From 1609 - 1691 it was held by the Poyntz family who adhered closely to the Roman Catholic faith after the Reformation. They sheltered and supported a priest, Dom Philip Powel, using their own private chapel in the south wing. Dom Philip Powel was eventually betrayed and then executed in 1645. The chapel still exists in a detached building behind the farmhouse. Leigh Barton, when under the monastic influence, had its own fishponds, mill, tile quarry and limekiln.

Today, apart from the more normal farm pursuits in evidence all around, the ancient barns house a modern example of diversification without which many such units might struggle to survive in the present adverse economic climate. **BRENDON HILL STOVES (01984 640238)** *use the outbuildings to house a large number of wood-burning and multifuel stoves. It is open on Monday to Saturday from 10 a.m. to 1 p.m. and 2.00 p.m. to 5 p.m. Visitors are welcome and cannot fail to appreciate the surroundings.*

Opposite the farm and barns, cross a grassed area to a gate leading into a conservation area in the trees. Follow the path as it skirts a pond, through another gate emerging into a field where it joins a farm track. There is a good view all the way down the field. A stile (with a slate step to help) gives access to the next field and here the path contours round until it reaches a hunting gate. Go through this one and pass straight down the middle of the field – the farmer leaves a good channel in the middle of his crop for this purpose. The gate in the bottom leads into a lane where another gate on the LH goes into a little pasture. The path tracks down the RH hedge, through a gate, past the house on the LH and out into the road. A RH turn will bring you back to the car park.

[Walked in July]

Walk No.19

[PERFECT IN SPRING, SUMMER AND AUTUMN TOO!]
Graded : EASY
Special features ~ Oaks and conifers

ST 033 366   2¼ miles [3½ km]   1¼ hours
Leighland to Hook Hill, returning via Pit Lane and Pitt Mill.
The walk is called 'Winter Walk' because most of it follows the
little lanes which, unlike boggy fields in winter time, give a firm
footing even when conditions are very wet. There are one or two
places by the river where you may need to choose your path
carefully but for most of it, whatever the weather, you will be dry.
Other seasons of the year bring just as many delights in this
peaceful part of the parish, springtime being especially beautiful.
🚐 At the first junction after The Valiant Soldier Inn at Roadwater,
take the LH turning, signposted Treborough and Brendon Hill.
½ mile up the hill take the first turning left to Leighland, reached
after 1 mile. 100 yards past St. Giles' church a new church car
park has been made on the LH (opposite Leighland Barn).
Marked 'Private', your car may be left here by kind permission of
Leighland Parochial Church Council (unless there is a church
function in progress in which case the car park may be full).

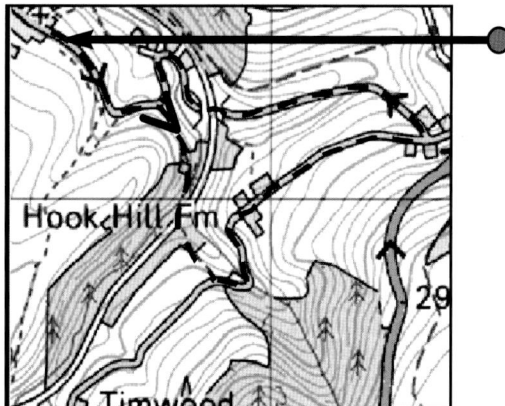

START: Walk on down the little lane for about ¼ mile. On the way you will pass a double gate and fingerpost pointing up to the RH – this footpath goes to Leigh Barton. Pass this by and a little further on, after passing some fir trees lining the road, the first of the massive veteran oak trees that feature in this walk rises out of the LH hedge. The trunk is huge and the tree towers above the lane. It must support a vast number of life-forms – insects, birds and plants. Just beyond this tree on the bend of the lane, the footpath leads off to the RH through a gate.

Once in the field you can see that it is in fact an orchard, planted with a number of apple trees. Follow the path round the top of the orchard (passing one gate on the RH) down to another gate. Through the gate, a few yards on, the path divides – take the lower LH arm and continue down the steep slope.

Some of the trees are Norway Spruce, Picea abies, native to the mountains of Scandinavia and north-west Russia. The timber, known as white wood, or deal, is used for roofing, house interiors or paper pulp. Turpentine is extracted from the stem but the tree is perhaps best known in Britain as the Christmas tree.

At the bottom, Pit Cottage hides in the greenery and the path skirts the property along its wooden fence and down to the river.

The river here is formed from the springs rising above Comberow and The Incline draining into this valley. The water, quite a torrent in winter, continues on down to join the Washford River.

Cross the river by the bridge and then 25 yards further along, cross a tributary by another bridge - narrow but with a handrail for safety.

The first tree on the RH as you enter the little wood ahead is a Western Hemlock, Tsuga heterophylla, a native of North America with interesting purple-brown bark. The foliage has a strong aromatic smell when crushed. In the autumn the damp undergrowth is peppered with numerous forms of fungi all thriving in the shady moist environment. Amongst these can be found the powdered white projections of the Stag's Horn or Candle-snuff Fungus.

Once in the wood turn almost immediately LH up some steps let into the earth – these bring you straight out onto the wide, and often muddy, track of the Mineral Line. There are no fingerposts to help with directions. Cross the Mineral Line and follow the footpath leading up the other side between the fir trees.

These trees are Sitka Spruce, Picea sitchensis,- important timber trees because they produce high-quality timber very quickly. They are native to the coast of western N. America and thrive in areas of high rainfall. The needles are spined at the tip making foliage prickly. The cones, 2-4 inches long, are distinctive with wavy-edged scales, and feel soft when squeezed. Each cone is a work of art – far beyond human skill to replicate. If you take one to pieces you can see how perfectly the scales, which hold the seeds, are set in spirals and how cleverly the seeds are released when the cone ripens.

Keep the stream on your LH as you go up the slope. At the top of the slope a hunting gate leads out into a meadow. 50 yards further up you can see a house – this is Lower Hook Hill (previously called Dorniford - now restored and renamed). The path <u>appears</u> to go along the bottom hedge towards the house.

<u>It does not</u>. The public right-of-way leads forward from the hunting gate for 50 yards, then veers to the RH straight up over the slope to another hunting gate and stile on the edge of the wood - these come into view as you contour upwards. The open grassed area in front of the house is a private garden so please do not venture forward or off the path. Dogs must of course be on leads.

The owners are working to promote wildlife, leaving their meadows for flowers and encouraging birds, bats and bees. A pond below the house is a haven for dragonflies and supports a variety of aquatic life such as frogs and toads. In this very special and unspoilt environment, the least we can do is to tread quietly and leave nature to prosper in its peaceful sanctuary.

Once over the stile and in the lane, turn LH and walk down past the farmhouse, round the corner and on up the lane.

Beeches line the beginning of the lane then later, on the LH, can be found some more of the magnificent oaks that are such a feature of this area. One very knarled oak has an open hollow trunk.

The autumn colours of these trees, the shades of yellow and gold, can be seen from miles away and when this turns to a rich bronze just before they lose their leaves they look as if they are on fire! The next house on the RH is Hook Hill Farm (error on modern O/S maps marks 'Hook Mill').

Hook Hill is listed as being of architectural and historical interest. It is a late 16th century/early 17th century farmhouse which is said to have a stair turret, chamfered beams and a cruck roof.

A little further on Mill Reef Farm on the LH is run as a small riding centre catering for local people.

The field just past the farm is called Loom Close and over the hedge the resident horses can be seen happily cantering around.

A pleasant ¼ hour's walk along the lane, towards Chidgley and the Sticklepath, brings you to Wilhay Farm. Just past the farm turn LH down the hill into Pit Lane.

Walk down the narrow sunken fern-lined lane, which is just wide enough for vehicles but you would be unlucky to meet one. After about ½ mile, at the bottom, pass under an arched bridge which carries the old Mineral Line over the road, and then on to Pitt Mill. Alders line the bank and the leat trickles along to the waterwheel. Continue up the hill past Pitt Farm after which you will very soon arrive at the fingerpost on the LH which marked the beginning of this walk, thus completing the circle. Continue the short distance back to Leighland and if you came in one, collect your car.

[Walked in December]

Norway Spruce
Picea abies

Sitka Spruce
Picea sitchensis

92

Walk No. 20

Graded : MODERATE
Special features ~ Waterfall and Mineral Line Incline

ST 029 353   3¼ miles [5 km] 1¾ hours
Comberow to the waterfall, on to The Incline and return.
🚌 At Washford Cross (Tropiquaria) take the turning to Ralegh's
Cross. After Chidgley, ½ mile up the Sticklepath, turn RH to
Timwood. Follow the lane almost as far as Comberow, park at a
RH clearing made for forestry work. Alternatively, from Roadwater
walk up the Mineral Line and follow the track to Comberow.

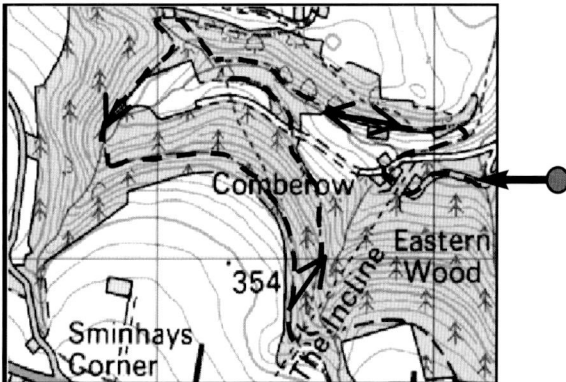

START: Walk along the road passing a new house on the RH and
passing under the Mineral Line's stone arch. Go through a gate
into a compound where horses are kept. A fingerpost by the far
RH house points to 'Ralegh's Cross by Waterfall'. Take this and
follow the path over the river, as the path climbs, turn LH. The
path goes steeply upward through the trees bearing slightly to the
LH and then the way becomes more obvious. Within a short
distance this path joins a wider track, and levels out. Fifty yards
on take the LH fork at a junction descending to the stream below.
The path passes some very large beech trees and keeps parallel to

the stream for a while before leaving the watercourse and going uphill for about ¼ of a mile.

When the path reaches a T-junction, turn LH following it downhill passing a small derelict cottage on the LH. Notice the bread oven on the LH end but please heed the following warning:

Do not be tempted to enter as the building is very unsafe.

Cross the stream and continue on a track edged by mature beech trees. The path bears to the RH and leaves the deciduous trees behind as it enters a coniferous section - this is the lower end of Western Cliff Wood.

The conifers include Douglas Fir, Pseudotsuga menziesii, Larch, Larix decidua and Norway Spruce, Picea abies. Some are magnificent specimens supporting a variety of birds and insects but the thick layer of pine needles is a death knell for plants.

However, it all changes again and the path continues in the open for a while with the sound of the waterfall increasingly apparent.

On the LH a meadow can be seen through the trees, while above, a buzzard quarters the skies and silently swoops into the undergrowth. All these central seaward-facing slopes of the Brendons are drained by the Washford River. On the upper outskirts of Roadwater the river fishtails into the hills with one branch spiralling round the natural bowl that is Comberow. From the rim of the bowl, which drops 800 feet in 1000 yards, a dozen small streams thread their way down through the trees to join up around Comberow and so form the eastern branch of the Washford River. One of the biggest streams runs down beside The Incline itself. Another stream begins below Sminhayes. After a short distance it slides 40 feet down an almost vertical moss encrusted rock face to make it one of Exmoor's more spectacular waterfalls. This is the Comberow waterfall that you are now seeing. While you pause here, you can often hear goldcrests at the top of the pine trees. Their song a high-pitched cheep - a 'tsee, tsee' in a descending series ending with a trill. This is one of the smallest European birds (the firecrest is the smallest). Goldcrests are olive green, with a brown tail, wings brownish with a double white wing bar. The crown stripe is yellowish gold in the female and flame-coloured in the male.

Leaving the waterfall behind, the path, which is more like a forestry track, contours round the hill, eventually climbing up through Forehill Wood turning RH at a fingerpost (Raleghs Cross 2) until a while later you can see that you are at the top of the wood and fields appear on the RH. A short downhill section brings you to a path junction. A right turn will bring you down on to The Incline.

The West Somerset Mineral Railway connected the port of Watchet with the mines of the Brendon Hills. Work started in May 1856 and by December 1857 had reached Comberow. To reach the summit, 800 ft above, a gigantic incline had to be built, three-quarters of a mile long at a gradient of 1 in 4. The difficulties of building this immense incline are illustrated by the rock cuttings, which show the drill holes made for blasting. Opened in May 1858 it was finally completed in March 1861. The mining venture at Comberow ceased in 1910 and the incline is now in the ownership of the Exmoor National Park Authority. Plans are afoot to grant public access in the future following necessary clearance work.

Return to the footpath, turn RH and go downhill – a long steeply descending track brings you to the lower slopes. Eventually you climb down a steep bank onto a track with a gate on the RH. *The track the other side of the gate going through the field is not a public right-of-way but provides access for the farmer.*

The footpath continues downwards through the wood with yellow waymarks painted on trees at intervals. At the bottom the path nears the river but veers off to the LH and climbs upwards for a while. After 200 yards the paths narrows to a defile abutting a wall eventually arriving at the river. Cross this (in winter you might have to find a shallower spot) and continue up the track to a junction with a bigger track. Turn RH and walk along beside the river (it can get very waterlogged after serious rain).

After about ½ mile the track is joined from the LH by the one coming from Leigh Barton. 50 yards further on it bisects again and here yellow waymarks are visible going to the RH. A few minutes walking downwards brings you back to the houses of Comberow and a little further along your transport home.

[Walked in August]

Walk No. 21

Graded : MODERATE
Special features ~ St.Peter's Church, Treborough,
and St.Giles' Church, Leighland.

ST 012 364   2¾ miles [4¼ km]   1¾ hours
Treborough Church to Leighland Church, returning to
Treborough via Leigh Barton Farm.

🚌 From Roadwater, take the left fork at the first signpost past the
Valiant Soldier Inn, to Treborough and Brendon Hill.
1½ miles up the hill, Treborough is found by turning right off
the Brendon Hill road. There is sufficient room for parking at the
side of the road.
(Times for walks do not include time spent visiting churches).

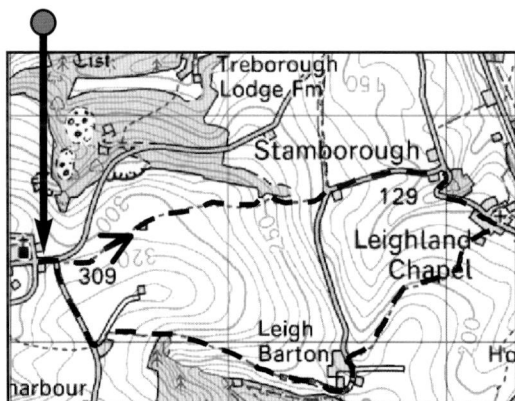

START : Walk along the road, turn right and take some time to
visit St.Peter's church which lies on the left in a uniquely tranquil
setting.
*It is noted as being probably the third-highest church in all Southern
England, suggesting that the site is of great antiquity, and in fact, the
first Rector was inducted in 1322.*
*The church is perpendicular in style, except the pyramidal tower roof,
which is 19th century. There is a 500 year-old ornamental font, a*

*medieval piscine and a wooden pulpit older than the Reformation. The
churchyard has a 13th century stone cross and in one corner is re-
interred a pre-historic skeleton whose slate-lined grave was uncovered
in Langridge Wood in 1820 under a small round barrow dating from
1500-2000 B.C. The barrow is situated 1200 yards NNE of the
Church. In the north churchyard wall a small engraved stone marks
this interment.*

Return through the settlement and cross the Roadwater to
Brendon Hill road and directly opposite the Treborough turning
go through the gate - the fingerpost is inside the field. Head for
the far hedge in the direction the post indicates keeping along
the lower side of the field and pass through a gap in the opposite
hedge. Make for the gate to the left of a shed which appears
opposite in the lower LH of the next field and you find you are
in an animal enclosure so if there is stock present, take care. Go
through the first gate immediately on the LH into another field
(no signs anywhere!) and follow the RH hedge down the field
passing one gate on the way.

*The view ahead is of Glasses Farm with a long view down the
Roadwater valley. Ahead on the skyline, in line with the next gate,
is the familiar landmark of Kingsdown Clump.*

Go through a wooden gate and walk straight ahead. A gap
appears in the hedge in front, guarded by a holly tree on its RH.
Through the gap into the next field there are no directions as to
which way to go. Make for the corner of the woods (taking a line
just to the LH of Kingsdown Clump on the horizon), noticing
Wood Advent Farm nestling in the hill directly in the
background. In the corner you will find a stile joined to a metal
gate. The stile leads into a wood, which may be difficult to access
because of the undergrowth. Here you make your way down the
slope for about 25 yards to join the main path skirting the wood
edge. When you reach it, turn RH between two big oak trees into
a dip and the stile can be seen 50 yards ahead. A notice points
out that there is a 'Bull in field.' This may or may not be the case
but it is quite safe to enter as it is not permitted to allow a
dangerous animal to be in a field through which a footpath runs.
Go over the stile into the field and downwards to the lower

hedge and into a second field.   Leighland and St.Giles' church
come into view. Keep to the LH hedge all the way to the gate at
the bottom.

Over this gate you will find the road from Stamborough to Leigh
Barton and on the LH a sign depicting 'Private Road'. In fact this
is a public footpath and if you should wish to take a short cut
back to the car follow the footpath to the main road, turn LH
and after a mile walking up the hill you will be back at
Treborough.

However, intrepid walkers pass the 'Private Road' sign on your
left and then proceed immediately down the hill. Turn RH at the
bottom of the hill and follow the lane down a shady dip and up
again the other side - the stream and pond at the bottom arise
from a spring near Leigh Barton on the RH hillside. As you turn
the corner into Leighland, St.Giles' church is ahead on the LH
side. This is the second of the two churches visited on this walk.
*The monks of Cleeve Abbey may have erected the first chapel here,
which survived the suppression of the abbey in 1539. By his will of
1611 Robert Poyntz left money for the maintenance of the chapel and
in 1791 it was described as a small chapel of ancient times belonging
to the parish of Old Cleeve. It was then a small structure of 46 feet
long and 19 wide, with a turret and one bell. During the busy mining
days in the Brendons, Leighland was formed into a separate
ecclesiastical parish and the chapel completely rebuilt in 1862 with
seating for 220 at a cost of £1,200. Constructed of local red sandstone
in the Early English style it now consists of a south porch, bellcote,
nave and chancel and was returned to Old Cleeve parish in 1955.
Members of the small community take great care of their large church,
and as well as the regular services, celebrate St.Giles' Day, the patron
saint's anniversary, with a pets' service held in the churchyard each
year at the end of August.*

Inside the church there is an excellent visitors' leaflet.

After your visit to the church come out of the gate and turn RH.
Almost immediately on the LH you will see a fingerpost pointing
up a grassy lane beside the cottage. Follow this path up through a
gate and into a meadow and walk up the LH hedge (this is a
dairy farm and the cows are friendly). Go through a metal gate

and then a RH wooden gate with a sign saying 'All dogs on lead'. A concrete trough marks the beginning of the footpath across the field and the farmer leaves a wide swathe through the crop for walkers. At the top is a hunting gate, marked ENP, and through this the path contours round the field. Another gate and stile appear, note the slate step, (from Treborough quarry?) to aid you over the stile.

The track follows the line of the RH fence and soon Leigh Barton, surrounded by trees, appears ahead. Just after a gate in the RH fence the path diverges to the right into a little grassy path, easily missed (ignore the main track which appears to go LH on up the field). Keep to the fence-line until you reach a semi-hidden gate into the wood. Through the gate there is a pond. This is a wildlife conservation area and after walking round beside the pond the way out through a gate leads into the farmyard of Leigh Barton. *Information on Leigh Barton is given in Walk No.18.*

Turn LH up the farm track, pass a turn to the left and continue up the lane. Pass by the first LH gate (fingerpost) and keep to the right of the slurry puddles, which are deceptively deep. Pass a second LH gate (signed - 'Please shut gate - ENP') and straight ahead is a double metal gate across the farm track. Through this the vista begins to open out and when through the next gate into the field, called Long Cliff, a house named Windwhistle can be seen ahead on the horizon with Broadfield Wood below on the LH. *Here on the sloping field, a number of stonechats are busy and goldfinches are enjoying the marsh thistles. As you walk up the field, you can hear the waterfall somewhere off to the LH.*

A ten-minute uphill slog brings you to a muddy junction where a gate leads into a sunken lane, fern-lined and cool. At the top of the lane turn LH on to a well-surfaced track and pass by Windwhistle just before you reach the road, then a RH turn leads back to Treborough. *Immediately opposite Windwhistle there is a good view over a field gate of distant Dunkery Beacon at 519 metres high, it is Exmoor's highest point.*

It is only ten minutes down the road before you are back in Treborough and your transport home.

[Walked in June]

Walk No. 22

Graded : MODERATE
Special feature ~ Parish boundaries and the old Sticklepath

ST 041 347   3 miles   [4³/₄ km]   1³/₄ hours
Sticklepath – (Old English) sticol : steep
From the Sticklepath to the junction of Galloping Bottom Lane
with Windwhistle Lane, on to Chidgley, returning via
Windwhistle Lane.
🚐 Take the B 3190 road from Washford Cross, to Ralegh's Cross
and Bampton. Keep straight on until you reach Chidgley (3
miles) and continue up the Sticklepath. Just as you reach the
crest, pass a large lay-by on the right - drive another few hundred
yards (4¹/₄ miles from Washford Cross) and you will find a small
lay-by on the LH by some field gates. Fingerpost - Chidgley 1³/₄.
(The building shown on the map has now gone.) This is a
bridleway, and a system of Exmoor National Park's blue
waymarks is helpful on the way.

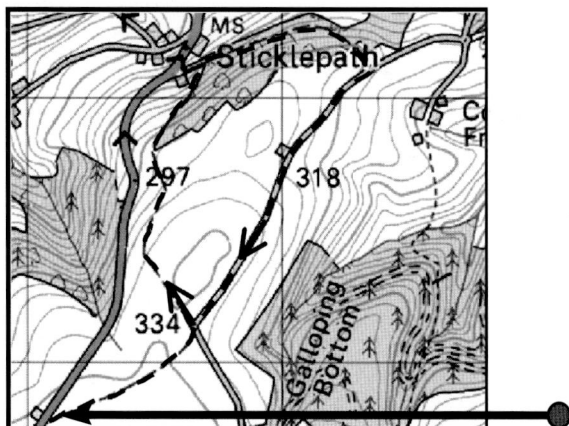

START: Enter the field and cross straight over to the far end of
the RH hedge – this hedge forms part of the southern boundary
of Old Cleeve Parish - a hunting gate will appear as you proceed.

Go through the hunting gate; follow the path along the fence on the LH noting underfoot some large lumps of quartzite, remnants of iron mining in the locality. Gates and a road ahead mean that you have reached Five-Ways, the junction of Galloping Bottom Lane and Windwhistle Lane.

The bridleway sign points LH to Chidgley and the path leads through another hunting gate and then keeps to the RH hedgeline.

An old drystone wall lines this field, remains of the furthest easterly section of Old Cleeve parish's boundary with adjoining Nettlecombe parish. The wall is habitat to a host of plants including Navelwort (Pennywort), Umbilicus rupestris, with distinctive round fleshy leaves. The wall was constructed in a traditional way using layers of local stone placed on their edges.

As you follow the wall, blue waymarks are visible at intervals, some painted on trees, and later the Sticklepath can be seen on the left. Go through a second gate (at present an open metal one) past some lone oak and beech trees onto a grassy track. The track merges with one coming from the left and this is the track of the old Sticklepath. *The complete track of the old Sticklepath is clearly defined on the Ordnance Survey map of 1809 together with the route of the new.* The bridleway follows the contours around the field - a hillock on the LH edge topped with rotting logs makes a useful viewpoint. *From the far left to right (north to south) is Brendon Hill, then Treborough Hill, Dunkery Beacon, Croydon Hill, Withycombe Hill and Minehead. The RH presents a good view of Kingsdown Clump's crest of trees. The small fields of West Somerset are laid out in a pattern on the slopes below, shaped generations ago and still, fortunately, part of our landscape heritage.*

Keep the hedge and wall on the RH as you continue on towards a scrubby patch of gorse and through a gate. The gorse increases and the path descends to another gate (gap in the hedge on the RH leads upwards to Beacon Hill which you are skirting). Little clumps of Bell Heather, Erica cinerea, appear indicating the acid soil and underfoot there are outcrops of shale bedrock.

Pass through yet another gate as you enter the wood finding among the native trees along the path some good specimens of the Sweet Chestnut, Castanea sativa. Follow the steep ferny path downwards passing a borehole and water-supply collecting tanks on the RH.

Please keep on the track. The wood is in private ownership and the bridleway passes through what is in effect part of the wild garden of the cottage below. Signs of work in progress are apparent as you walk downwards and in the treetops a family of goldcrests twitter amongst themselves. Below on the LH, there is a further section of the old Sticklepath which came straight up the hill in a steep line.

A short distance ahead, the bridleway is joined by a track leading from the B3191 road just above Chidgley. At this junction a fingerpost provides directions.

If you make a detour of a few yards back towards the road you can see the above-mentioned cottage nestling in a bower of trees. This building was erected in 1790 by the estate owners at Nettlecombe on the actual line of the old Sticklepath in order to restrict free passage. A new road was built, the present Sticklepath, and this was turnpiked. It is said that local people could squeeze behind the cottage and use the old road to avoid paying the toll but, the story goes, had to pay for a draught of beer at the cottage door.

Back at the fingerpost follow the path to Monksilver and Colton. *Signs of deer and badgers can be seen if you examine the muddy track. Some more magnificent mature trees edge the path – further specimens of sweet chestnut intermingle with tall oaks and beeches. Chidgley Farm can be seen below and windows appear in the wood giving a variety of views.*

The path continues and just as it comes to a gate on the left you can make out another section of the parish boundary, which comes down a raised bank on the right. Ahead a fallen beech bough arches over the path - you are now in Nettlecombe parish with the Old Cleeve parish boundary dropping away to the left hand of the gate below.

This part of the hillside was in full view of Nettlecombe Estate and was landscaped to fit in with the rest of the park. This landscaping was done by Messrs. Veitchs of Killerton, near Exeter, celebrated nurserymen of their day, and no doubt accounts for the different type of planting in this end of the wood.

Should you be here in early spring, a carpet of bluebells provides the last touch for a perfect setting of a truly English landscape.

The bridleway leads uphill through the wood towards Windwhistle Lane with a new vista on the left away to the Quantock Hills and Staple Plain.

Soon the path crosses a wide forestry track and a few paces ahead comes to a gate. In the field keep to the LH for 50 yards, then cross to a gateway in the opposite hedge and thus into Windwhistle Lane.

Turn RH into the road and walk upwards.

The lane is empty of traffic but lined with wild flowers even in autumn, including red campion, willowherb, toadflax and bramble, plus a quantity of the rather attractive but rampant alien, Himalayan Balsam, Impatiens glandulifera. As you walk up the lane the view through any of the LH gateways shows Galloping Bottom to the right and serried ranks of clone-like conifers cloaking the hillside.

Continuing upwards note Windwhistle barn on the RH – this is a traditional barn with its old pillars and arched doorways still intact although sadly the slate roof has gone. Empty and neglected it looks as if it would make a happy home but the name of the lane might give second thoughts even if the planners would permit!

Rabbit holes line the roadside banks and provide interesting habitats for certain mosses. One, a luminous moss, Schistostega pennata, grows in mine workings and old rabbit holes. It is less than ¾ inch high but gives out a green luminescence as you peer into the depths - a sort of natural fairylight. It has been found on the Brendons - although not recorded at Windwhistle it could be here.

20 minutes on the road (30 if you investigate all the rabbit holes) brings you back to Five-Way. Just before you reach the gates on the RH, note the parish boundary on both sides making a 'pinchpoint' in the road. Presumably, in former times, this entrance to Nettlecombe parish would have been gated at the point where it left Old Cleeve parish.

Retrace your steps through the gate ahead along the bridleway. It is ten minutes over the fields to the Raleigh's Cross road and your transport.

[Walked in October]

NAKED BOY

Walk No. 23

Graded : EASY (with all level ground)
Special Features ~ source of River Tone and Burrow Engine House

ST 015 345   2 miles [3¼ km]   1¼ hours
Naked Boy to Beverton Pond and returning, with the inclusion of
a diversion to Burrow Engine House.
🚐 From Ralegh's Cross, take the B 3190 towards Bampton, turn
right onto B3224 at Brendon Hill Methodist Chapel, also called
Beulah Chapel. 50 yards after a RH turning to Treborough, turn
LH into an unclassified lane just before Sminhays Cottage.
*100 yards up the side-road Naked Boy's stone can be seen on the left of
the roadside. Made of quartzite, this single standing stone has become
the boundary mark between the parishes of Old Cleeve and Brompton
Regis and it denotes the highest and most southerly point of Old
Cleeve Parish. It is listed as being a medieval stone of historical
interest. Naked Boy's stone stands on the line of the ancient
Harepath, which runs from east to west along the length of the
Brendon Hills and Exmoor. The Harepath starts at the junction of two
other ancient roads at Triscombe Stone on the Quantock Hills. From
Elworthy Barrows it follows more or less the line of the tarmac road
along the ridge of the Brendons.*

There is adequate room for vehicles to park opposite the stone.

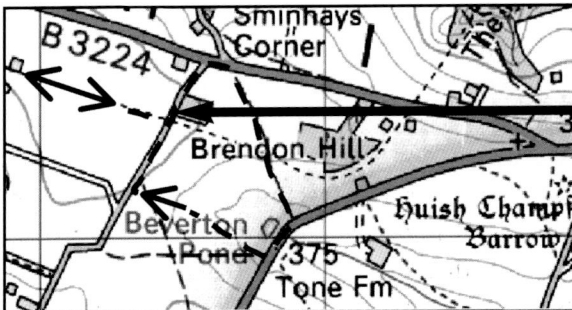

START: Walk down towards the B 3224 - *on the RH hedgebank there is a patch of wild raspberries, Rubus idaeus.* Turn right at the T-junction, going along the road for a short distance, past the turning to Treborough, until there is a gateway into the first field on the RH(fingerpost - Bridleway). Cross the field to the gate in the middle of the opposite hedge (front left) – even in summer this can be very muddy as the field is used for stock. The path opens out into a wide avenue of beech trees and crosses over the disused track of the West Somerset Mineral Railway. Pass through a gate, and continue down the avenue. After a short distance of easy level walking through the leafy tunnel, the road is reached.

This is Point A – a suitable track for wheelchair users and those with children in pushchairs to walk up the path into the beech woodland. There are no views but it is a very peaceful safe area for children to play and a delightful setting in which those less mobile could enjoy wildlife and tranquillity amidst the trees. Point A can be reached by road by driving from Ralegh's Cross westwards and after ½ mile taking the LH turning to Bampton on the B3190. Point A is ½ mile further on.

The swampy area where the springs rise is the source of the River Tone. Named Beverton Pond, it is visible on the right. Birds and plants inhabit this wetland area – mallard swim quietly among the rushes and dragonflies and damselflies are plentiful.
Turn RH along the road – this is now Brompton Regis parish and a fast road leading to Upton and Bampton. The footpath leads into the RH field adjoining the pond and technically crosses into the middle of the field where it meets one coming from the other direction and in a dog-leg returns to the other end of the hedge. In reality, especially if the field is full of sheep, the RH hedge line

will take you to the next gate. *The map shows a * tumulus site in the top LH corner of the field.*

Soft rush, Juncus effuses, in the grass, indicates the underlying water and the boggy ground makes heavy going. At the far gate turn RH into the road that leads back to Naked Boy.

OPTIONAL ADDITION

Provided you can lift the pushchair over the stile, the walk to Burrow is suitable for pushchairs. A little way down the road towards Naked Boy a fingerpost on the left points to a permissive path leading to Burrow Engine House.

There used to be a bridge here crossing the public road. Called Naked Boy's Bridge, it was demolished to avoid the cost of future maintenance when the mineral railway was abandoned.

Pass over the stile and down some steps onto a level grassy path that runs above the derelict track of the West Somerset Mineral Railway. After a good ½ mile of level easy walking, the ruins of the Engine House are reached and a permissive path leads to the site. Exmoor National Park Authority has placed an information board at the side of the building explaining its history.

Burrow Engine House is the better preserved of the two surviving today (the other being at Kennesome Hill). It was built around 1880 to the design of Captain Henry Skewis, the Cornish Mines Captain, and housed a 25-inch combined pumping and winding beam engine.

Return along the grassy pathway to the road, turning LH and so back to Naked Boy.

[Walked in April]

If you turn left onto the B 3224 at the end of Naked Boy lane, you will find Sminhays Cottages – this was a terrace of miners' cottages. Today, the RH end (No.3) houses a rural cottage industry, **Brendon Hill Crafts, (01984 640939)** - *Telephone for appointment. An unusual diversity of products, such as paintings, prints and preserves, are supplied to shops and enterprises locally and as far away as Cornwall's Heligan Gardens. The fruit used in the jams is grown locally and the preserves can also be bought from other local outlets such as Washford Mill. If you call, you will find a welcome from the busy owners, David and Liz Jessup.*

Walk No. 24

Special feature ~ Parish traverse from most southerly point (Naked Boy's Stone) to most northerly point (Blue Anchor sea front) using definitive paths and the minimum of road connections.

Graded : CHALLENGING
ST 015 315   8 miles [13 km]   4 hours
From Naked Boy's Stone by footpath and road to Sea View Farm, then footpath to the incline. Down to Comberow, up to Leigh Barton and Leighland, then down 'The Rocks' to the Mineral Line. From Traphole to Glasses Farm, Tacker Street in Roadwater over the hill to Croydon and down to Golsoncott. From Forche's Garden down Forche's Lane to Bilbrook, across the A39 and up to Old Cleeve. Through the village, down Church Path to Binham, over the fields to Home Farm (delicious celebratory tea in the tearoom) and the last few yards to the sea front.
🚐 Logistics for this walk suggest a lift to the beginning – athletes may prefer to return to collect their vehicle retracing their footsteps in an uphill direction – all the way!
A map is provided for the first part of this journey as far as The Incline – all other footpaths have been described in full in the text relating to other walks and are noted as you require them.

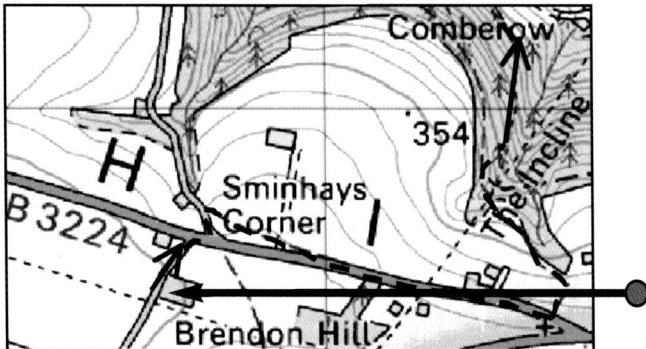

START: Walk down towards the main road leaving Naked Boy's Stone in its lonely setting. Cross the road watching for speeding vehicles, and turn down the road signposted Treborough.

The next section may seem a little pointless as it would be possible to follow the road towards Ralegh's Cross but a) it is an exceedingly fast At least you are the other side of the hedge. b) This is the last of the footpaths in Old Cleeve parish and so including them uses up all the definitive rights-of-way and completes the book.

Before the Treborough road turns a corner a gate on the RH leads into a field. In this field take an upward and rightward direction almost to the road. The footpath tracks over the field and should have crossed into the next field a little way down. However, a new fence means that in effect you have to use the gateway to gain access to the next field and here the footpath follows the hedge along running parallel to the road. At the end of the field a gate takes you out to the road. The next 250 yards has, unfortunately, to be undertaken on the road edge. Fast traffic can make this miserable, but there are a few pull-ins to help. One of these is a wide entrance marking the top of The Incline and the winding house.

The Incline and the winding house now come under the auspices of Exmoor National Park Authority. At present the winding house is being restored not having been touched since it was partly rebuilt in the 1930's. The winding house contained two drums 18 ft (5.5m) on an axle. Steel cables raised the empty trucks up the incline using the weight of iron ore going downwards. After the mines closed, once in 1883 and then finally in 1910, the machinery was removed, the shafts sealed and the buildings left to fall into ruin.

During the First World War the rails were commandeered for scrap by the Ministry of Munitions with the land auctioned off in 1924.

A little further on the imposing Sea View House can be seen set back from the road. This was the residence of the Mine Captain and overlooks The Incline. Its most famous occupant was Morgan Morgans. Once this lonely house has been passed there is not much further to go on the road.

Turn LH at the next gateway and follow the LH hedge down the field following it right round the corner and through a gate into an area of rough grass planted with trees.

A pond on the RH has a skirt of rushes and a (stone?) heron perches artistically on the hem.

Follow the hedge onwards down the slope and into the wood. Turn LH, walk a little further and you are on the slopes of The Incline.

*The Incline is crossed by a rutted pathway and looking downwards you can see it is a haven for flora especially ferns and shade-loving plants. The Incline is described in **Walk No. 20 - Comberow.***

Before you enter these woods it is a help to remember that all paths eventually take you where you want to go even if you go round in a complete circle! Do not worry if you go in another direction or even if you are not sure where you are – at some point you will find the right path or a useful waymark.

Cross The Incline, follow the path up through the wood, take the LH track up the hill to the hedgeline in front, at which point the path turns RH and starts to descend. Follow it down the slope until it bisects. Follow the RH branch leading down through the wood, crossing forestry tracks at different points and noting the yellow waymarks. The path slopes steeply down onto a farm track, cross this and slightly on the LH the path continues through the trees until you reach a grassy meadow. Cross the meadow and exit by a stile immediately opposite. Bear LH and join a track leading over the river on and uphill through the wood until it joins the path leading from Leigh Barton to the waterfall. Turn RH and in a short distance you will arrive at Leigh Barton.

Turn RH and walk down through the farm buildings as far as the Conservation Area on the RH - see **Walk No. 18** - Leigh Barton, which will lead you over the fields to Leighland.

Once in Leighland turn LH and then immediately RH down past the old school. At the bottom turn LH along the footpath and down the 'The Rocks' to the Mineral Line. Walk along the Mineral Line for about ½ mile until you pass the Traphole treatment works. Here reverse the instructions in **Walk No.14** - Valiant Soldier Walk.

Turn LH up the footpath and over the fields to the road. Turn RH and then a few yards on, LH up the steps into the fields above Glasses Farm. Traverse the fields and come down the steps onto the Luxborough road. Almost opposite, a little leftwards go down the lane into Tacker Street and from here reverse the instructions in **Walk No.12** - Felon's Oak.

Go over the river, up through the wood, into the field then follow the RH hedge all the way to the barn. Turn RH and enter the lane leading to Croydon Hall. Pass the hall entrance and turn RH along the track and through the houses. This leads out into parkland below Croydon Hall and following instructions in **Walk No 11** - Croydon Walk - make your way through Golsoncott to Forche's Garden.

Turn in at Forche's Garden, walk RH down the grassy path and bear LH into the woody lane, which tracks down to Bilbrook using the reversed directions in **Walk No. 9** – Forche's Lane.

Cross the A39 into Bilbrook Lane and walk past the ford. At the railway bridge, go up the footpath and on into Old Cleeve village. Just before the church lychgate, take the lane down (No Through Road) and follow it out onto Church Path. Cross the field diagonally to Binham Cross and thence over the road and down to Binham Farm. Reversing the instructions in **Walk No. 3** - Black Monkey - will take you out to Home Farm at Blue Anchor (just in time for tea!) and thence to the sea wall where Old Cleeve Parish ends.

This is only one of the numerous ways that it is possible to walk from Naked Boy to Blue Anchor. There must be at least a dozen or so alternatives using different footpaths. The satisfaction of walking within the parish is enhanced by the prospect of such diversity.

You can do it over again tomorrow and the next day, ... and all on different footpaths! A joy for all who find pleasure in walking.

[Walked in September]

Marine snail shell
Peringia ulvae

110

APPENDIX 1

A list of publications consulted during the writing of this guide.

New Flora of the British Isles, *C.Stace. Cambridge University Press.*

The Moss Flora of Britain and Ireland, *A.J.E.Smith. Cambridge University Press.*

A Field Guide to the Trees of Britain and Northern Europe, Alan Mitchell. Collins.

Butterflies & Day-Flying Moths of Britain and Europe, *Michael Chinery. Collins.*

The Minehead District, a concise account of the geology, *R.A. Edwards. British Geological Survey. The Stationery Office.*

Cleeve Abbey, *R. Gilyard Beer. HMSO. (plus assorted handbooks from English Heritage).*

Birds of Britain and Europe, *Jim Flegg and David Hoskin. New Holland Publishers Ltd.*

The Story of Roadwater *compiled by members of the WI. 1953.*

The Church of St.Peter, Treborough, *E.F. Williams, Luxborough.*

St. Giles', Leighland, A Short History. *(No author)*

Nettlecombe Court: The Trevelyans, *R.J.E. Bush. The Buildings, G.U.S. Corbett. Field Studies. The Invicta Press.*

A History of Watchet, *A.L.Wedlake. The Exmoor Press.*

Exmoor Microstudies: *The Exmoor Press.*
 Churches and Chapels of Exmoor, *N.V. Allen.*
 The Waters of Exmoor, *N.V.Allen.*
 The Old Mineral Line, *R.J.Sellick.*
 The Trees and Woods of Exmoor, *Roger Miles.*
 Antiquary's Exmoor, *Charles Whybrow.*

APPENDIX 2
WSDC RIGHTS-OF-WAY IDENTIFICATION NUMBERS
All the following rights-of-way are designated as footpaths unless,
(BR) Bridleway or (RUPP) Road Used as a Public Path

WL18/1	Blue Anchor sea front to Pill River
WL18/2	Pill River through to Binham Farm
WL18/3	South-west of Huntingball Wood to Watchet road
WL18/4	South-east of Huntingball Wood to Watchet road.
WL18/5	From coastal path through Warren Bay to Watchet road
WL18/6	Cleeve Hill north of The Priory to Watchet road
WL18/7	South of Jenny Cridland's Copse to Kentsford Farm
WL18/8	Tuck's Brake to Washford recreation ground
WL18/9	Binham Farm to Old Cleeve/Blue Anchor road
WL18/10	Binham Cross to Old Cleeve via Church Path
WL18/12	From Black Monkey to Withycombe parish boundary
WL18/13	Old Cleeve (Rockleigh) to Bilbrook railway bridge
WL18/14	Bilbrook over White's Meadow to Dragon Cross
WL18/15	Steps Farm, Bilbrook to Whitley Brake
WL18/16	Bilbrook Cottage via Forche's Lane to Whitley Brake
WL18/18	Lodge Lane via Lodge Rocks House to Forche's Lane
WL18/19	Forche's Lane to Thistlewell and Golsoncott road
WL18/20	Lodge Rocks to road south-west of Gracepits Copse
WL18/21	Lodge Rocks east to join 18/22 near Trowden Wood
WL18/22	Washford Garage by Trowden Wood to Lodge Lane
WL18/24	From 18/22 to St.Pancras Chapel and river (unusable)
WL18/25	Road at Torre to Bardon (section unusable at Torre)
WL18/27	Washford Station behind Castle Mead to Railway bridge
WL18/28	Washford School to Willow Grove (part of Monks' Path)
WL18/29	From railway bridge to Monks' Path – Cobbler's Steps
WL18/31	From field kissing gate through Belle Vue estate to A39
WL18/33	(BR) Higher Hayne, to Leighland (The Rocks)
WL18/34	Leighland Chapel through Pitt Mill to Pit Wood
WL18/35	Leighland (path plus spur at beginning) to Comberow
WL18/36	Leighland Chapel to Leigh Barton Farm
WL18/37	Road above Pit Cottage to Dorniford (Lower Hook Hill)
WL18/38	Mill Reef Farm to Pit Lane at Mineral Line bridge

WL18/39	(BR) Chidgley through Pit Wood to Roadwater
WL18/40	Chidgley Manor Farm to Nettlecombe parish boundary
WL18/42	(BR) Sticklepath to 5-Way, Chidgley and Windwhistle
WL18/43	Chidgley Hill Farm towards Kingsdown Clump
WL18/44	Stamborough to Treborough parish boundary
WL18/45	Leigh Barton Farm to join 18/47 in Broadfield Wood
WL18/46	(BR) Leigh Barton to waterfall and top of Incline
WL18/47	Three paths in Broadfield and Market Path Woods (Two are footpaths and one is a bridleway)
WL18/48	(BR) Higher Sminhayes Farm to Brendon Hill road
WL18/49	(BR) Sminhayes to parish boundary near Beverton Pond.
WL18/50	Bottom of Batallers Lane to Thistlewell
WL18/51	Roadwater Farm to junction with 18/50
WL18/52	Roadwater Farm to Mount Lane
WL18/53	New Barn, Golsoncott to Roadwater (by Church)
WL18/54	Golsoncott to Greenland Lane, Croydon
WL18/55	Felon's Oak to Mount Lane, Roadwater
WL18/56	Roadwater (near phone box) to Mount Lane
WL18/57	Tacker Street, Roadwater to 18/55 at Croydon
WL18/58	Glasses Farm to Traphole on Mineral Line
WL18/59	Roadwater through Road Wood, south to Ham Lane.
WL18/60	From Road Wood to Lower Hayne
WL18/62	Warren Bay along cliff path to Blue Anchor road
WL18/63	(RUPP) Leigh Barton to Treborough parish boundary
WL18/64	Railway Line up Cleeve Hill to Watchet road
WL18/65	(RUPP) Black Monkey Bridge to parish boundary
WL18/66	Treborough road to Stamborough
WL18/67	Golsoncott Lane to Thistlewell
WL18/68	Greenland Lane to barn and junction with 18/57
WL18/69	Top end of Forche's Lane to junction with 18/19
WL18/70	(RUPP) Wilhay Farm to Pitt Mill (Pit Lane)
WL18/71	Lower Hayne on Mineral Line up to Ham Lane (RUPP from Ham Lane to river at junction with 18/60)

Paths 18/11, 18/17, 18/23, 18/26, 18/30, 18/32, 18/41 and 18/61 no longer exist, disappearing at the 1954 Rights of Way Survey.